Architecture of Skidmore, Owings & Merrill, 1997–2008

[signatures]

2009.12.08

Architecture of Skidmore, Owings & Merrill, 1997–2008

Introduction by Kenneth Frampton

The Monacelli Press

Library of Congress Cataloging-in-Publication Data
Skidmore, Owings & Merrill.
SOM : architecture of Skidmore, Owings & Merrill, 1997–2008 / introduction by Kenneth Frampton.
p. cm.
ISBN 978-1-58093-224-0
1. Skidmore, Owings & Merrill. 2. Architecture—United States—History—20th century. 3. Architecture—United States—History—21st century. I. Title. II. Title: Architecture of Skidmore, Owings & Merrill, 1997–2008.
NA737.S53A4 2009e
720.92'2—dc22   2009022203

Printed in China

www.monacellipress.com

10 9 8 7 6 5 4 3 2 1
First edition

Project Editors: Elizabeth Harrison Kubany and Landis Livingston Carey

Project Texts: Sara Moss

Design: Pentagram Design Inc.

Contents

SOM at the Millennium: A Provisional Critique
Kenneth Frampton

Throughout the best part of its existence, SOM has been renowned as the ultimate corporate practice, even though a considerable number of rival mega-offices have come into being since its foundation in 1936. However, none of these rival firms has ever been able to lay claim to SOM's all but mythic reputation as a practice capable of serving the establishment over a broad front, that is, responding with equal skill to the very different demands of administration, finance, speculation, and military power.

SOM's modus operandi, as much a performative standard as a seemingly self-effacing style, was for many years virtually inseparable from the ethos and methods of the Illinois Institute of Technology, that equally renowned Chicago institution, the architectural faculty of which was first assembled, under the leadership of Mies van der Rohe, in 1937, one year after the fledgling practice of Skidmore & Owings began to build its progressive reputation. It would not be long before Mies's graduate students began to infiltrate the firm, bringing with them the precept of "almost nothing," which was as much about the rhythmic expression of high-rise steel-frame construction as it was about the tectonic articulation of the glass skin with which such structures were invariably enclosed. Paradoxically, this minimalist, neo-Miesian syntax, which became the signature of the practice, enabled a succession of exceptionally talented designers to distinguish themselves from one another by inflecting the received "objective" code to suit their individual capacities and temperaments. Despite this differentiation, a certain laconic line prevailed in the separate SOM offices until the late 1950s when, as Henry-Russell Hitchcock has observed, there was a discernible shift in the aspirations of the office, which seems to have been initiated by Walter Netsch's design for the Air Force Academy Chapel. Irrespective of its ecumenical stance, the pointed form of this structure—Gothic by association—announced a decisive break with the trabeated order of the campus by which it was surrounded.

An equally audacious departure from orthogonal rationalism came with Chuck Bassett's John Hancock Building in San Francisco, a twelve-story, four-square, curtain-walled prism with pierced windows situated on top of a vaulted, reinforced-concrete undercroft. This split with the restraint of the late Chicago manner would be followed by variations on the structurally decorative potential of prefabricated-reinforced-concrete construction as devised by Gordon Bunshaft for both the Banque Lambert in Brussels and the Beinecke Library in New Haven. These works were in process exactly a decade after Bunshaft's minimalist, curtain-walled Lever House, New York (1952). From this point onward, SOM would continue to vary its expressive manner according to the character of the context and the nature of the institution, frequently anchoring the free-standing result in a well-formed civic space.

Its origins notwithstanding, the heterogeneity of SOM makes any balanced assessment of its recent production difficult to achieve, in part because of the diverse character of the firm, with offices in London, New York, Washington, Chicago, San Francisco, and Shanghai, and in part because of fundamental shifts in scale, location, client, and brief between one project and the next. Thus, any kind of provisional overview requires a taxonomy with which to differentiate genres from one another or, alternatively, to pass from one mode of beholding to another. Hence, in the text that follows, I have elected to survey the work under the selective rubric of five different categories: span, height, topography, media, and the tectonic.

Span

As Viollet-le-Duc implied in his *Entretiens* of 1872, the greatness of a civilization may be gauged by its capacity to achieve a large span. While SOM had few occasions to pursue such a tectonic ambition during the second half of the twentieth century, the firm would finally have an occasion to do so in the Atlantico Pavilion, realized on the banks of the Tagus River in Lisbon by the London office in 1998. With its clear span of 380 feet, this gigantic volume accommodates an elliptical tribune capable of seating 12,500 people, plus a multipurpose space for an additional 2,000. Sixteen laminated transverse timber trusses support the overarching shell, which is also fabricated from timber. The aerodynamic profile of this roof, cantilevering at its eaves beyond the perimeter glazing, was inspired by the profile of Vasco da Gama's sailing ships, which once berthed in the harbor. Like that through the hulls of these ships, the longitudinal section through the roof is slightly asymmetrical, with a prow that protrudes beyond the entry to the north. At the same time, the expressive sweep of the glass louvers beneath the eaves of the standing-seam roof echoes the streamlined form of the seaplanes that once plied the river.

It is hard to imagine something more removed from the simple elegance of this single shell than the triple-span tubular steel truss adopted for the main hall of the International Terminal at the San Francisco Airport (2000). The authors conceived of this structure as the high-tech equivalent to a typical nineteenth-century rail terminus, thereby evoking in certain respects the prewar ethos of La Guardia Airport in New York. While it approximates a representational front on a scale that befits an international terminal, it does so in a manner that is somewhat ambiguous.

SOM also responded to the high-tech challenge with acuity in the International Arrivals Building at John F. Kennedy Airport, completed in 2001. The more ample site at JFK favored a more integrated parti with vehicular access for departures above and arrivals below. The two corresponding halls are layered in section so as to combine the straight eaves of the upper volume with the bowed front of the lower. As in San Francisco, the symbolic presence of the roof is reserved for the departures hall, which is covered by a 230-foot lattice truss of welded tubular steel, distantly recalling the arches of Renzo Piano's Kansai Terminal of 1994. A particularly felicitous move by SOM at JFK was to situate the concessions concourse one level below the departures hall so that its volume is symbolically associated with the same overarching roof.

The other recent SOM air terminal to be predicated on the concept of the large-span shed is Terminal 3 at Changi International Airport, completed as part of Singapore's airport complex in 2007. Here one is close to the spirit of Mies's gigantic space-frame for the Chicago Convention Center of 1953, although in this instance, the lower chord of the space-frame is covered by a louvered ceiling made up of perforated-aluminum panels that double as adjustable light baffles. However, departing from the tectonic emphasis of the late Miesian manner, the lightweight, ludic character of this span stems from the way in which the passage of the sun is mediated by the haptic play of its pivoting sun shades, which are activated by sensors.

Height

SOM's reputation in the 1960s was virtually inseparable from its then unrivaled capacity to refine the format of the neo-Miesian high-rise, of which Lever House was the supreme example. This minimalist prism in seamless green glass was one of the most exemplary works of the firm's early practice. Even so, it would appear in retrospect to have been a rather atectonic response to the challenge of the multistory building, a problem that had first been broached over half a century earlier in Louis Sullivan's Guaranty Building, Buffalo (1895), which first bracketed the skyscraper form into the classical subdivision of bottom, middle, and top. The Guaranty Building was rendered as a two-story base capped by a shaft of closely spaced piers that culminated in an Egyptoid cornice. This exotic exercise, faced throughout in ornamental terra cotta, led in short order to Cass Gilbert's neo-Gothic Woolworth Building of 1913 and thereafter, via New York's 1916 Zoning Resolution, to the stone-faced Manhattan Art Deco skyscrapers of the 1930s. The totally glazed curtain wall, which became economically feasible after 1945, promptly led to SOM's Lever House and to Mies van der Rohe's 860–880 Lake Shore Drive of virtually the same date. Where the former effectively suppressed the structural frame, the latter succeeded in expressing both shaft and frame.

All of SOM's high-rises of the late 1950s were subject to this inherent tension between the skin and the frame, with the office invariably tending to favor the structure, as one may judge from its masterly Chase Manhattan Bank, New York (1961), where the expressive verticality of the frame serves to emphasize the shaftlike nature of the slab. At the same time, in Chicago, SOM adopted a more equitable approach in the Hartford Fire Insurance Building, where a seven-by-nine-bay, reinforced-concrete frame was rendered as an articulate structure with haunched junctions at the intersections between beams and columns. In this case, the mullions of the glazing were set back from the face so that the horizontality of the spandrels and the verticality of the columns were equally well expressed.

SOM departed from variations on this paradigm by introducing the diagonally braced exoskeleton, which broke up the scale and height of its hundred-story John Hancock Center, realized in Chicago in 1970. Since the mullions of this work barely projected beyond the surface of the glazing, the only features that mediated and unified the repetitive fenestration were the cross-bracing of the frame and the tapering of the width of the structure as it rose. The final high-rise innovation during this pioneering period was surely the Sears Tower, completed in the same city in 1974 to the designs of Bruce Graham and Fazlur Khan. Here a radical, quasi-sculptural stratagem was employed to modulate the height: the cruciform plan of the 110-story structure steps back in increments in a spiraling formation about its central core.

The exoskeleton approach has reappeared recently in two medium-rise office complexes: Poly International Plaza, in Guangzhou, China (2006), and the 201 Bishopsgate and Broadgate Tower buildings in London (2008). The south sides of the twin slabs deployed in Guangzhou are diagonally braced by concrete brise-soleils that both stiffen the frame and shield the office space from the sun. A similar diagonal bracing inflects the skin of the London development, even if here the exoskeleton is virtually integrated with the skin. Of these two works, the rhythmic figure of Poly International Plaza is the more outstanding, not only because its dynamic form is more than fully complemented at grade by the spatial articulation of the three-story podium and landscape that grounds the two slabs but also because open-air belvederes are let into the body of each slab.

Lenovo/Raycom Infotech Park, completed in Beijing in 2004, is of a similar scale and genre. Here, as in Guangzhou, a medium-rise development is mediated by the creation of an urban enclave. The resulting sense of civitas is heightened by a totally glazed lobby that spans between the two seventeen-story, curtain-walled slabs that comprise the complex. The glazed, cable-stayed catenary roof of this space emphasizes the dematerialized character of the entire composition.

The eighty-foot lower portion of SOM's recently completed 7 World Trade Center high-rise is largely occupied by Con Edison transformer vaults; this form is covered by two layers of stainless louvers designed in collaboration with the engineer-artist James Carpenter. The double-layered relief engenders a random moiré effect depending on the position and movement of the observer, an effect that is enhanced at night by blue and white lights suspended within the cavity that separates the two layers of the screen. The abstract, haptic treatment finds a certain complement in a scrolling

LED installation by Jenny Holzer in the entrance foyer. Since the structural frame of 7 World Trade Center is suppressed, the seemingly infinite height of the building is unmodulated except for overlapping glass spandrels at each floor accompanied by mirror glass backing and a blue sill; the spandrels enliven the facade through an oscillating play of reflections that are variously activated by climatic conditions and the movement of the sun.

Equally minimalist fenestration unifies the form of the dark glass membrane enveloping the twin towers of SOM's Time Warner Center, completed on Columbus Circle in Manhattan in 2004. Possibly the most felicitous aspect of this striking composition is the way in which its skyline profile echoes the twin apartment towers that have long since punctuated the length of Central Park West. At the same time, the circumferential mass of the podium, faced in black stone, helps to confirm the overall character of the complex as a city in miniature, and this bestows on a salient point in the city fabric an aura of sophisticated urbanity that is rarely found in contemporary development.

Topography

Although SOM was to pioneer the suburban office park, until very recently landscape design was hardly a major focus of the office. This makes the current excursus into low-rise topographic form all the more significant, particularly as this is manifest in three schools designed by the New York office of SOM and realized in New England between 2002 and 2007. The first of these, a new upper school for the Greenwich Academy in Connecticut, represents a change in attitude on the part of SOM with regard to the expression of the standard steel frame, for in this instance, the frame is not only lined with laminated timber but also furnished throughout with timber fenestration. The judicious use of wood imparts to the whole an undeniable warmth that confers on the structure an atmosphere that is at once liberative and generous. Aside from this use of wood, three features of this school are especially striking. The first arises out of the unique characteristics of the site: the buildable area entailed a twenty-three-foot change in level between the old villa in which the school was originally housed and the playing fields, situated to the west of the site. The second feature derives from the attention to sustainability evident in the decision to cover the roof with turf, which has the effect of fusing the form of the building with the greensward that surrounds it on every side. The final distinctive topographic move was to collaborate with the artist James Turrell on the design of four light courts within the two-story depth of the structure. Aside from providing much needed zenithal light, these courts are equipped with LEDs that generate constantly changing emanations of color.

The second of the schools is the two-story Burr Street Elementary School, realized with a more limited budget on an equally bucolic site in Fairfield, Connecticut, in 2004. Here the center of the plan is occupied by a library/media center that opens onto an exterior courtyard. This kidney-shaped plan-form is the largest of four organically shaped atriums that bring light into the depth of the plan. The square format of the school is made denser on its flanks by single-story classrooms stacked on two floors throughout. Here and there, the upper level looks down to the ground floor through double-height spaces, some of which serve as extensions to the courts. The topographic nature of this work stems in the main from the organic shapes excised out of its mass and its northern and southern facades. Oblique views into the attendant woods afford a felicitous sense of being immersed in an all-encompassing unspoiled landscape.

The last of the three schools is the new Koch Center, completed in 2007, for Deerfield Academy in Massachusetts. Brought into being as the consequence of an interdisciplinary symposium, the science center fulfills an exemplary pedagogical program. This derives in large measure from features designed by SOM in collaboration with James Turrell and observational astronomer Richard Walker: the creation of a star field map, designed to show what the skies will look like in 2040, and an analemma skylight, which tracks the trajectory of the sun's rays over the course of a year. Both of these set pieces represent and complement the scientific orientation of the institution, along with its planetarium, growth garden, and biological laboratory.

Under the rubric of topography one must acknowledge the comprehensive urban/landscape proposals that have been generated by SOM in recent years, including a remarkable plan for Chongming Island in China and a total reworking of the corniche in Alexandria. The Chongming master plan (2004) is projected for an island at the mouth of the Yangtze River, close to the megalopolis of Shanghai. The plan consists of a series of linear transit spines running down the length of the island. The first of these is a central waterway, which affords a site for some forty agricultural villages. The second spine skirts the southern coast of the island and is planned to link eight regional cities that, along with the villages, will expand the current population of the island by some two hundred thousand. These conurbations will be linked to Shanghai by rapid transit and to the southern bank of the Yangtze by ferries. Aside from the improved transport infrastructure, this plan provides for the symbiotic integration of the wetlands with paddy fields, since rice cultivation is the overriding basis of the economy. The other compelling proposal of recent date is the project for upgrading the water-front of Alexandria, Egypt (2006). Here the viability of the proposition turns on the introduction of light rail along the full trajectory of the corniche. This circumferential strategy is carried further by a fragmentary landfill that provides a new breakwater for the harbor as part of a continuous green circle of movement running from the new library of Alexandria to an antique fort situated on a promontory at the entry to the harbor. What is especially notable about this project is the way in which the various components of the plan allow for its realization over a twenty-year period. Aside from the light rail and the tree-shaded promenade, no single element is crucial to maintaining the sense of civic continuity.

Media

SOM's evident propensity for incorporating environmental works by such distinguished artists as James Carpenter, Jenny Holzer, and James Turrell seems to have encouraged the firm to embrace, on occasion, a totally mediatic approach to architecture in which the built domain is superseded by a totalizing display of "cybernetic" imagery and signs. This is most evident at a large scale in the Jianianhua Center in Chongqing, China, completed in 2005, where the visual impact of the whole stems from rotating blades set behind a glass wall. This constantly changing display runs the gamut from giant advertising slogans to decorative multicolored patterns and incidental photographic images. The building is treated as though it were a piece of scripted civic decor, an aspect that is reinforced at night, when the rotating screens are backlit.

An equally hallucinatory effect is evident in two recent interiors realized in Manhattan in 2004 and 2006, respectively: the Skyscraper Museum downtown and the Condé Nast Cafeteria in midtown. Where the first is low-tech, static, and dependent for its dynamic aspect on the movement of visitors between the all but equally reflective surfaces of the floor and the ceiling, the second is high-tech and masterful, activated by the changing backlit luminosity of its bounding walls and suspended ceilings, lined throughout with opalescent glass and enlivened aesthetically by seventy thousand synchronized light diodes. The bulk of the space is suffused with a constantly changing light display, issuing from the walls and the ceilings, wherein the ambient color subtly alters its hue during the course of a coffee break or a meal. The dynamic display also changes the apparent color of the neutral furnishings, while movable panels provide for an occasional rearrangement of the space. These recent projects represent a conceptual threshold where the mediatic challenges the continued viability of architecture in se and where the dematerialization of the environment metamorphoses into an assembly made up of nothing other than the transitory effects of light, reflection, and color.

The Tectonic

It may be argued that the tectonic as "a poetics of construction" has always been a latent aspect in SOM's architecture, notwithstanding the stylistic shift in the ethos of the firm in the 1980s, when the work assumed a historicizing pastiche character. The tectonic first reemerges in the output of SOM at the millennium with such projects as a parametric space-frame galleria, the main iconic feature in a proposal to convert New York's Farley Post Office into the new Penn Station, dating from 1999, or the cable-stayed, cylindrical high-rise projected for the Qatar Science Center in Doha three years later. Additional projects in which overt structural expression was the dominant principle were envisioned at around the same time, such as the trussed floors of a bank headquarters projected for Marina Bay, Singapore, in 2001 or the cable-tied, Nervi-like, partly prefabricated, concrete roof projected for a subterranean transit system serving Dulles Airport, Washington, D.C., in 2002. One may add to these tectonic proposals various lines of technological research that have been pursued by SOM in recent years, such as the structural glass studies published in the first issue of the *SOM Journal* in 2001, or the rotating fusable joint, developed in 2004, a device that would allow steel-frame structures to deflect without incurring permanent deformation in response to extreme seismic conditions.

Such works may be seen as an indication of a more general return to what one might regard as the initial focus of the firm. While much of this design research has been facilitated by digitization, it should be noted that parametric methods may just as easily be used for decorative ends as for structural and ecological inventions of a more fundamental character. Thus, the technological only evolves into a poetics of construction under certain circumstances, as is demonstrated by the articulate detailing of the Central Plant Complex erected for the new University of California, Merced, in 2005. This seven-story service building is destined to play a fundamental role in reducing the energy consumption of the university by 20 percent over what is currently the norm. It accommodates under one roof not only the usual assembly of pumps, chillers, boilers, and cooling towers, all stacked on three levels, but also a seventy-five-foot-high cylindrical thermal storage tank capable of holding thirty thousand ton-hours of chilled water to meet the campus's cooling needs. The various parts of this structure are covered with a metal skin of varying configuration and porosity. At times, it is watertight, shingled and corrugated; at other times, it is louvered and open to the air. Below this metal sheath, a curtain wall of channel glass admits natural light while at the same time partially revealing the machinery within. It is just this play between revealing and concealing, between the ontological structure and its representation, that introduces the poetic element.

This tectonic sensibility emerges to an even greater degree in the nearby library and information-technology center. What is unusually striking in this work is the way in

which a trabeated, reinforced-concrete, columnar structure is shielded from the sun by large louvered screens in such a way as to create an unusually generous public space within the depth of the building. A major element in this work is a five-story breeze hall that, aside from picking up cooling winds off a nearby lake, affords a "space of public appearance" linking the two wings of the complex, the library on one side and the information center on the other. These spread-eagled structures are flanked by arcades and loggias at grade, which provide shaded walkways, while the building as a whole is louvered and fritted differently on each face to minimize glare and reduce solar gain. In addition to the white roofs provided throughout to reflect radiant heat, the buildings have been equipped with elaborate systems for the recycling of waste water. However, aside from the systematic reduction of its ecological footprint, what is tectonically impressive about this work is not only the way the structure articulates itself as a statical invention but also the way in which it serves to establish the honorific public character of the space within.

How to be modern and return to sources, as Paul Ricoeur once put it, is a challenge that remains current, along with certain sociopolitical aporia that tend to inhibit the critical realization of liberative form in our time. While SOM has responded to this challenge before, the rhythmic flair and feeling for the tectonic is especially marked in these university buildings.

When one looks back over the last decade of production, one is struck by the renewed rigor manifest in much of SOM's recent work, particularly with respect to certain building tasks that afford a social scope that is not available in the more instrumental commissions with which it has long been familiar. Thus as one may judge from this volume, SOM's strongest work is to be found in a spectrum that spans from the modern air terminal to the mid-rise office complex with multilevel, ground-floor commercial space. This spectrum may be expanded to include the layered, landscaped forms of low-rise school buildings, not to mention the recent topographic exercises in urban design. The varying range of topic and expression, the essential substance of the firm over more than half a century, is still the basis for the finest strains of the firm's recent production.

Skidmore, Owings & Merrill

Partners 1997–2008

Mustafa K. Abadan
Stephen A. Apking
William F. Baker
C. Keith Boswell
Leigh S. Breslau
Carrie E. Byles
David M. Childs
Raymond J. Clark
Roger F. Duffy
George J. Efstathiou
Peter G. Ellis
Philip J. Enquist
Thomas K. Fridstein
Carl E. Galioto
Joseph A. Gonzalez
T.J. Gottesdiener
Gary P. Haney
Craig W. Hartman
Roger G. Kallman
Thomas P. Kerwin
John Kriken
Brian Lee
Peter Magill
Jeffrey J. McCarthy
Michael A. McCarthy
Larry K. Oltmanns
Mark C. Regulinski
Peter M. Ruggiero
Mark P. Sarkisian
Gene J. Schnair
Adrian D. Smith
Marilyn Jordan Taylor
Richard F. Tomlinson II
Robert L. Turner
Anthony T. Vacchione Jr.
Jaime Velez
Robert L. Wesley
Ross Wimer
John H. Winkler
Carolina Y. C. Woo

Atlantico Pavilion
Lisbon, Portugal, 1998

Atlantico Pavilion takes its architectural cues both from its immediate surroundings and from ancient seafaring history. The structure, located on the Olivais Dock, was built for Expo '98. Its interior construction was inspired by the sailing ships of Vasco da Gama, the explorer whose fifteenth-century voyage to India was one of the themes of the world's fair.

The pavilion, kept low in order to harmonize with nearby buildings, is surrounded by curved concrete steps. The distinctive ovoid roof, clad in oxidized zinc, rests on a glass-walled vestibule. Inside are soaring spaces; the laminated wood beams, which span 115 meters, are visible, as is the warm timber ceiling. A three-thousand-square-meter hall seats up to 12,500 spectators around a six-lane, two-hundred-meter Olympic track. A smaller auxiliary hall with space for an additional five hundred to two thousand people may be used in a number of different ways, including as a warm-up area for athletes.

Operable skylights admit daylight and provide natural ventilation, and the concrete grandstands serve as a heat sink when the hall is filled to capacity. Cool air travels through low-velocity ducts to individual grilles underneath each seat, a strategy that consumes half the energy of conventional systems.

Site plan.
1 Main hall
2 Auxiliary hall
3 Vasco da Gama Tower
4 Tagus River

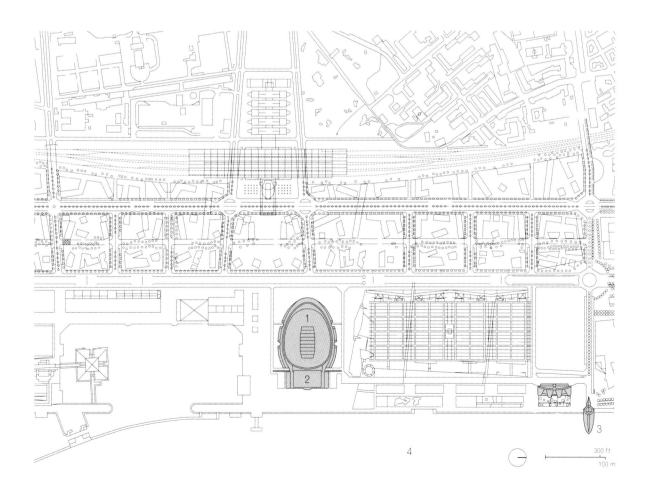

300 ft
100 m

View from the west. The roof of the pavilion
has a skin of ribbed zinc panels and sits above
19   a glass-walled vestibule.

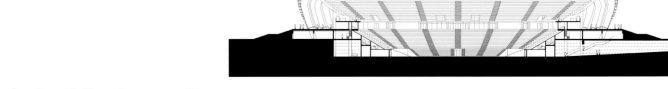

View from the south. The multipurpose pavilion was the main facility for special events at Expo '98 in Lisbon.

◁ View of the auxiliary hall, which has a large perimeter terrace with views to the river.

Sections. The rings of concrete steps outside create a fluid transition between building and ground. Visible in the bottom section are the skylight roof windows.

View of the circulation corridor at the perimeter of the arena. The interior structure resembles the hull of a ship, with long, laminated wood beams and a timber ceiling.

View of the skylight windows over the main arena. These can be shaded if necessary.

Plan, entrance level.
1 Information desk
2 Ticket booth
3 Foyer
4 Concession stand
5 Presidential box
6 VIP box
7 Permanent seating tier
8 Temporary seating tier

View of the arena. The seating is raked at a
shallow angle to enhance viewing and maintain
a low building profile.

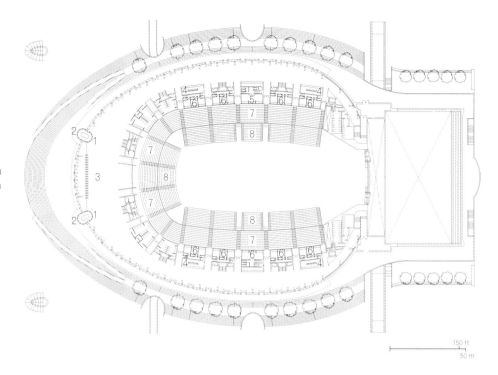

150 ft
50 m

101 Second Street
San Francisco, California, 1999

This twenty-six-story office tower in San Francisco's South of Market district responds to the modest scale and local characteristics of its neighborhood. The design concept reinterprets San Francisco's prescriptive building envelope for high-rises, which calls for a "wedding cake" building mass and a historicist interpretation of urban context. The 440,000-square-foot building achieves a slender profile by breaking the overall mass into a series of vertical volumes, each with discrete functional and structural roles.

Vertical circulation and building services are housed in the limestone-clad central shaft, which has punched windows and a glass veil at the top enclosing the mechanical equipment. This core provides lateral seismic and wind bracing for the adjacent glass-and-steel volumes, which contain the office space; their minimal frames maximize glazed areas to give tenants ample city views.

At night, the atrium and the crown are illuminated, calling attention to the building's presence on both street and skyline. At ground level, a glass art pavilion serves as the building entry as well as a naturally lit atrium open to the public. Pivoting glass panels along Second Street also provide access. The pavilion blurs the boundaries between public and private, bringing them together in a protected, four-season urban room.

View of the corner of Mission and Second ▷
Streets from the west.

Plan, ground floor.
A 101 Second Street
B Rapp Building
1 Public atrium
2 Lobby
3 Retail
4 Loading dock
5 Ramp up
6 Ramp down

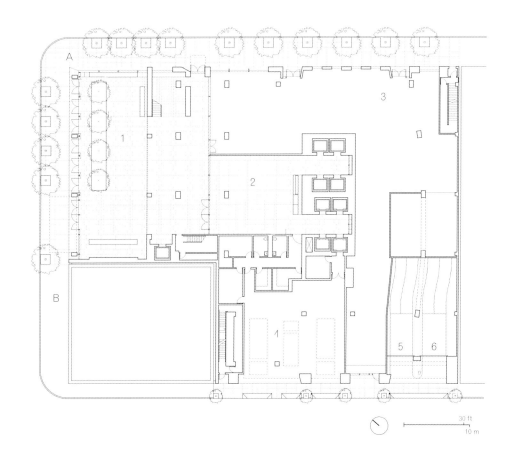

30 ft
10 m

View into the public atrium from Mission Street.

Northeast facade. Careful massing and a warm, earth-toned palette help the building respond to its urban context.

View from the east.

Section.
1 Typical office floor
2 Entry/Art pavilion
3 Elevator lobby
4 Lounge

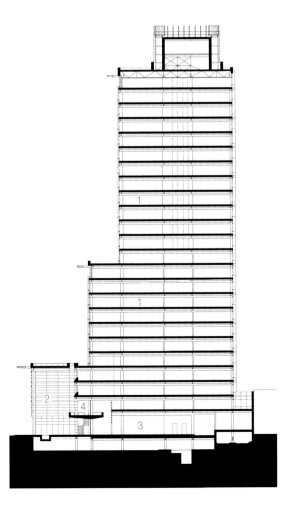

Street-level view of the public atrium. Pivoting glass panels open to the street and blur the line between public and private.

Plan, typical low-rise floor.

Plan, typical high-rise floor.

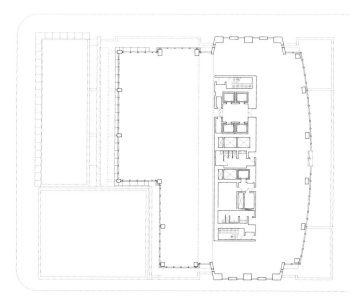

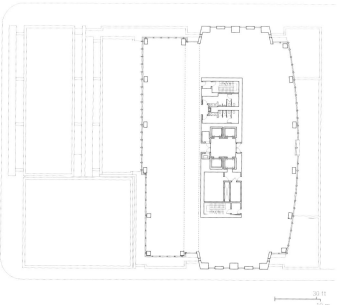

30 ft
10 m

View west from the atrium.

San Francisco International Airport: International Terminal
San Francisco, California, 2000

The centerpiece of the San Francisco International Airport's $2.6 billion expansion, the new International Terminal forges a visual identity through the integration of structural and architectural design. The terminal and its two adjoining wings comprise 1.8 million square feet and can accommodate up to five thousand passengers an hour. Its five-level vertical organization provides a model for other urban airports with constrained sites. The terminal's distinctive long-span roof structure allows the building to bridge existing access roads. The chords of the roof's double-cantilevered steel trusses resemble a double sine curve. Bowstring trusses link the roof trusses, and in the central span, they form skylight structures with light-diffusing fabric lenses. Lighting, heating, cooling, and ventilation systems are consolidated in the hall's freestanding ticketing islands so that the roof, unencumbered by services, acts as an enclosure that can admit natural light. The west facade of the terminal, of translucent and fritted glass, is both an entry facade for the airport and an iconic image for visitors to the city. Incoming daylight is filtered by the facade and then by a linear bamboo grove. Subject to demanding seismic requirements, the building incorporates base-isolation technology, which separates the structure from the foundation with a series of bearings. In the case of an earthquake, the bearings allow the building to move as a single entity.

View of the west facade. Passengers enter ▷ the departures hall on the third level. The distinctive roof is formed by double cantilever steel trusses.

Site plan.
1 International Terminal
2 U.S. 101
3 San Francisco Bay

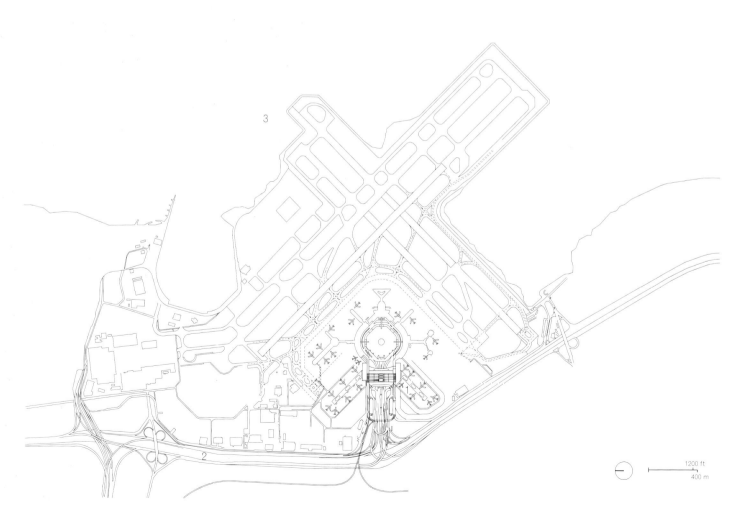

3

2

1200 ft
400 m

View of the west facade from the roadway that connects the airport with U.S. Highway 101. The roof structure spans 825 feet and soars at 115 feet above the third level.

Sections.
1 Departures/ticket hall
2 Baggage claim
3 Meeters/greeters hall
4 Baggage area
5 Inbound/outbound roadway
6 Mechanical
7 Office

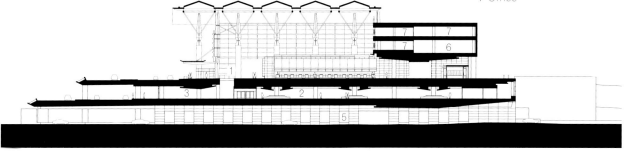

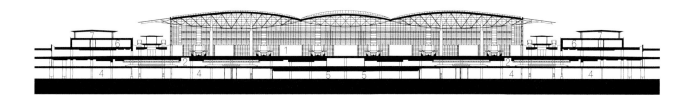

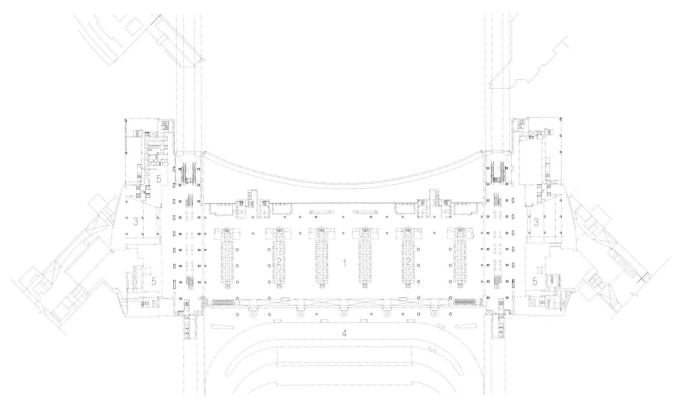

Plan, third level/departures and ticketing area.
1 Departures/ticket hall
2 Airline ticket counter
3 Security checkpoint
4 Departures roadway
5 Retail

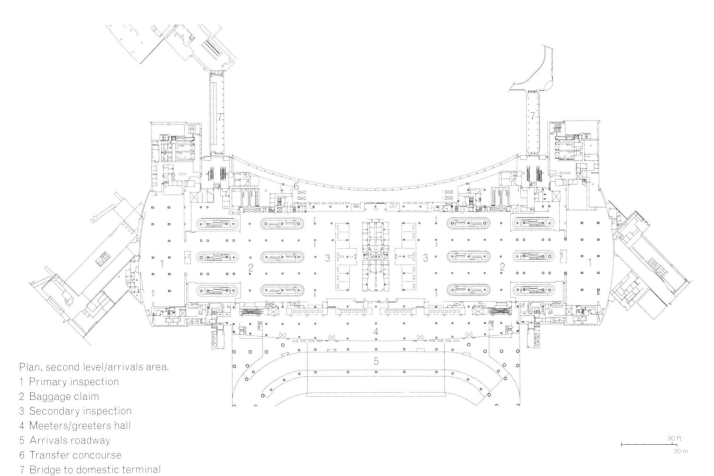

Plan, second level/arrivals area.
1 Primary inspection
2 Baggage claim
3 Secondary inspection
4 Meeters/greeters hall
5 Arrivals roadway
6 Transfer concourse

7 Bridge to domestic terminal

90 ft
30 m

View of entry walkways along the west side of the arrivals hall. A linear bamboo grove diffuses the strong sunlight entering through the west facade of the main hall.

Detail view of the connection between a roof truss and a column capital.

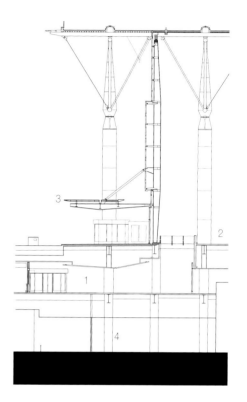

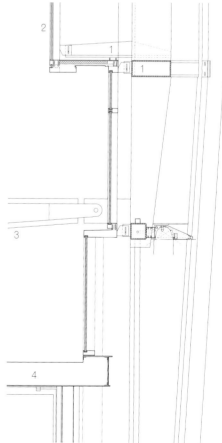

View of the ticket counter in the departures hall. Above are airline offices.

◁ Section at entrance.
1 Greeters hall
2 Departures hall
3 Entry canopy
4 Tour group lobby

◁ Detail, wall section.
1 Curtain wall support structure
2 Curtain wall
3 Entry canopy
4 Entry vestibule

View of the bowstring truss skylight structure. The skylights incorporate a light scrim artwork by James Carpenter.

View of the intersection between the roof structure and the cherry wall of the office building (fourth and fifth levels).

Pages 36–37:
The main departures hall. The six ticketing islands contain lighting and mechanical systems so that views are not obstructed.

Changi International Airport: Rail Terminal
Changi, Singapore, 2001

This large rail terminal provides a pedestrian link between Changi International Airport's Terminals 2 and 3 as well as access to the city's rapid transit system. The station spans the distance between the terminals—nearly three hundred feet—and consists of a below-grade platform; tall atriums at either end admit natural light to the interior. The centerpiece of the station is a long-span bridge that is also an important lighting and wayfinding element.

Each 130-foot-high atrium has a concrete core on the north end and a steel frame on the south that support the roof. At the glass facade is a slender cable-truss system. Spanning between the atriums is the 650-foot bridge, at the time of its completion the longest clear-span pedestrian bridge ever built. The bridge, clad in translucent glass with internal illumination, serves as a mezzanine level and the primary source of light within the station. Because of the bridge span, the train platform is free of columns.

View of the glass-enclosed south atrium. The ▷ skylight in the foreground admits daylight to one end of the train platform.

Site plan.
1 Terminal 1
2 Terminal 2
3 Terminal 3
4 Rail terminal
5 Airport Boulevard

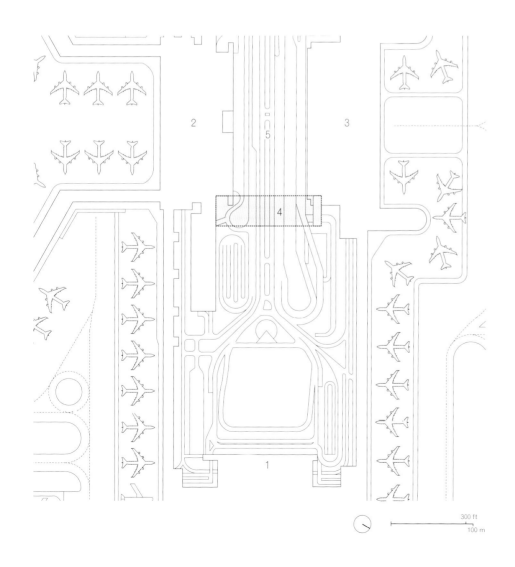

300 ft
100 m

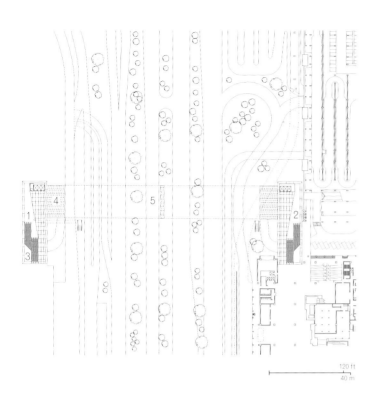

Plan, ground level.
1 North atrium
2 South atrium
3 Terminal escalators
4 Skylight
5 Airport Boulevard

Plan, bridge level.
Plan, platform level.
1 Platform
2 Tracks
3 Turnstiles
4 Control booth
5 Glass bridge
6 Moving walkway
7 Open to below
8 Garden
9 Platform elevators
10 Platform escalators

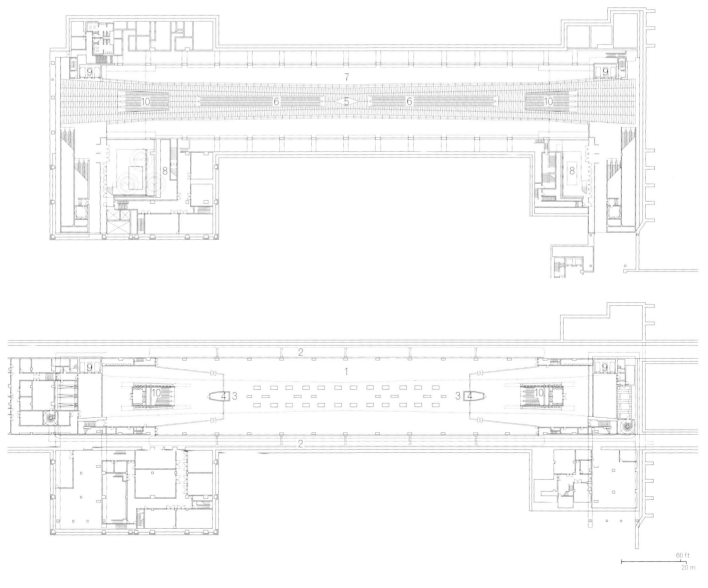

The parabolic long-span bridge.

View down the 650-foot-long glass bridge, which serves as a pedestrian connection between Terminals 2 and 3.

View of the south atrium from the departures level of Terminal 2. The translucent-glass bridge is visible at the bottom of the image.

View of escalators to the underground station, which are housed in the glass-enclosed atriums.

Interior detail of the atrium facade. Stainless-steel props support the double-glazed wall and connect to one-inch-diameter vertical steel cables. Secondary stainless-steel ties provide diagonal bracing.

North-south section.
Typical east-west section through atrium.
 1 South atrium
 2 North atrium
 3 Airport Boulevard
 4 Skylight
 5 Escalator access to platform
 6 Escalators to terminal
 7 Bridge
 8 Elevators to platform
 9 Rail tunnel
10 Double-glazed wall

Pages 44–45:
View of the south atrium from the departures level of Terminal 2. Stainless-steel-mesh louvers provide sun shading and allow for air movement within the double-glazed wall, reducing heat gain in the space.

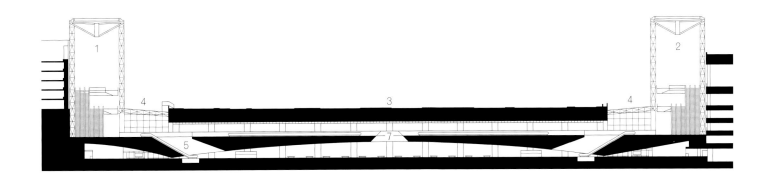

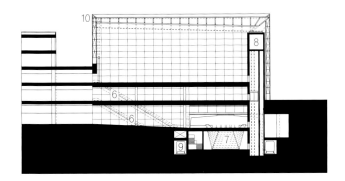

Charles Schwab Investor Center Prototype
New York, New York, 2001, 2004

Part of a major brand repositioning, the prototype Investor Center offers a new retail environment and graphic identity for Charles Schwab and provides a consistent, holistic customer experience that may be adapted to specific locations. The approach incorporates space planning, interior architecture, signage, technology, and furniture to create a corporate image for the organization, which had many outposts but no unified retail identity. Two locations in New York City—a prototype on Park Avenue and a flagship in Rockefeller Center, part of the national rollout—serve as models for the company as a "full choice" financial services firm, emphasizing advising and trading capabilities.
The open interior is simple and uncomplicated to allow the layered branding to be visible. Visitors are offered a clear choice of all available services, from curb to front door to financial adviser, in a seamless experience. Large-scale graphics establish a presence in the streetscape that reinforces brand messaging.

The reception area of the Park Avenue prototype.

Plan.
1 Reception
2 Waiting area
3 Investing terminals
4 Quick advising
5 Senior advising
6 Meeting room

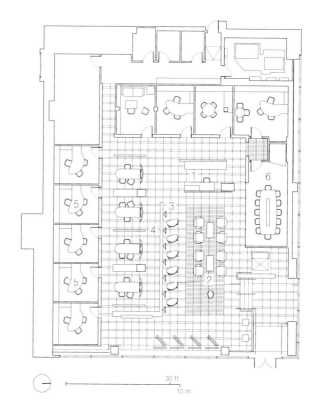

30 ft
10 m

Night view from the north of the Rockefeller
Center Investor Center. The design standards,
including billboard-like signage, may be adapted
to various settings.

John F. Kennedy International Airport: International Arrivals Building, Terminal 4
Queens, New York, 2001

The new $1.2 billion Terminal 4 at John F. Kennedy International Airport replaces the 1957 International Arrivals Building, also designed by SOM. The 1.5-million-square-foot, three-level terminal serves seven million passengers per year, provides larger, more flexible facilities, and will accommodate future expansion. Its design recalls the tradition of great civic transportation facilities, creating an expansive central space with abundant daylight and views of the airport's activity. Various permanent artworks enliven the terminal's interior spaces.

Fully glazed on both landside and airside, the terminal creates a connection between airport, street, and runway. Passengers have clear views of the checkpoints in the departure and arrival process as well as of the aircraft, control tower, and surrounding apron. Linear skylights admit natural light, reinforcing the simplicity and clarity of circulation. The roof of the departures hall is a lightweight, 180-foot-long span; the hall underneath is a column-free space. This open area allowed flexibility in the layout of interior components, including the ticket counters, which are oriented to facilitate airfield views.

A multilevel retail court at the junction of the concourses and the terminal core provides a central point of activity close to the gates. The new two-pier concourses accommodate sixteen gates. A two-level roadway serves arriving and departing passengers, and an intermediate level inside the terminal incorporates a station for JFK's light-rail system, which links to other terminals, remote parking, the New York City subway, and the Long Island Rail Road.

Site plan.
1 Parking
2 Arrivals roadway
3 Departures roadway
4 VIP parking
5 Service/loading dock
6 Terminal
7 Concourse A
8 Concourse B
9 Air traffic control tower
10 Hard stands

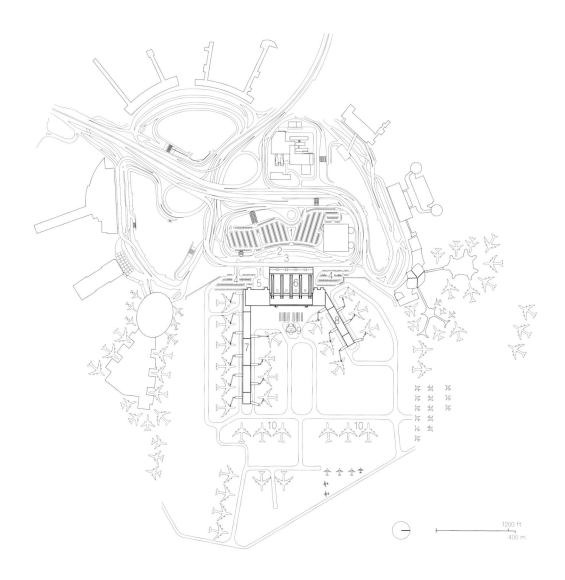

1200 ft
400 m

Night view from the north, with departures
hall at top and arrivals hall below.

View of the upper-level entry to the departures hall.

Sections.
1 Departures curb
2 Departures hall/ticketing
3 Light rail
4 Retail
5 Customs/immigration
6 Baggage claim
7 Arrivals hall
8 Ticketing hall beyond
9 Mechanical room

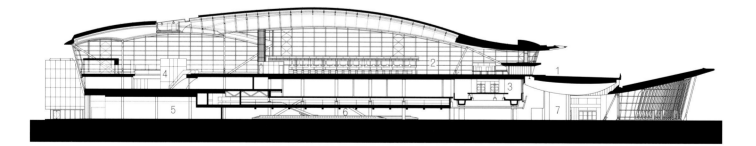

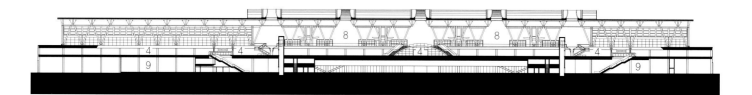

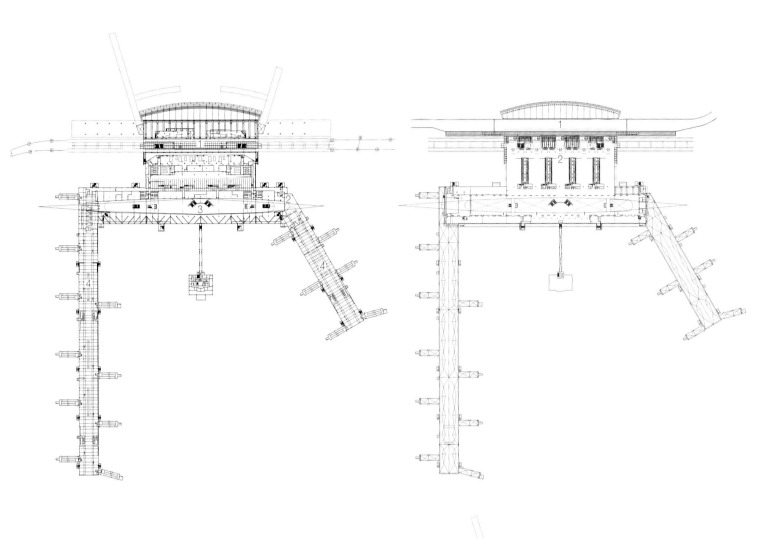

Plan, third level/retail and gate lounges.
1 Light-rail station
2 Security
3 Retail
4 Gate lounges

Plan, fourth level/departures.
1 Departures curb
2 Departures hall

Plan, first level/arrivals.
1 Arrivals curb
2 Arrivals hall
3 Baggage claim
4 Customs
5 Inspection

300 ft
100 m

View of the immigration hall. Deborah Masters's band of relief sculptures, *New York Streets*, is located above the booths.

◁ The departures hall. The roof design allows for generous daylighting and reinforces circulation.

View of the departures hall. Alexander Calder's mobile *Flight*, designed for the original terminal building, was restored and reinstalled.

View of the corridor between arrival gates and immigration. *Travelogue*, designed by Diller + Scofidio, consists of a series of lit lenticular panels with images that evoke travel.

Pages 54–55:
View of the check-in area.

Lever House: Curtain Wall Replacement
New York, New York, 2001

Designed by SOM and built in 1952, Lever House was one of the first glass-walled International Style office buildings in the United States. An early example of sealed-glass construction, the iconic skyscraper set a precedent for establishing corporate identity through architecture.

Thirty years later, the Landmarks Preservation Commission designated Lever House an official landmark, and fourteen years after that, in 1996, the commission granted approval for the replacement of the curtain wall. By that time, due to weather and age, only one percent of the original glass remained. In addition, the structural system of the facade required a thorough overhaul.

The existing vertical-steel-post support system was cleaned and, where necessary, replaced. The steel glazing channels, which had deteriorated, were removed and replaced by identically dimensioned aluminum channels. The aluminum channels hold vision glass in place with neoprene gaskets, replacing the outdated wet-glazed system. The glass was replaced by identical quarter-inch-thick Solex vision glass to maintain the original design intent.

The signature shadow-box spandrel detail was replaced with a new assembly of quarter-inch heat-strengthened blue-green glass with a chrome-green metal backing panel, re-creating the visual effect of the original facade. Anodized aluminum louvers and stainless-steel coping covers were reused where possible; elsewhere, new components made of the same materials were installed.

Due to changes in construction methods, every element of the curtain wall was moved out by a quarter inch. While the exterior is minutely larger, the singular components of the building are fundamentally unchanged.

View from Park Avenue looking northwest. ▷

View of Lever House in 1952, the year of its completion.

Restored podium corner.

View from east across Park Avenue. All of the original glass has been replaced with visually identical glass that meets energy requirements.

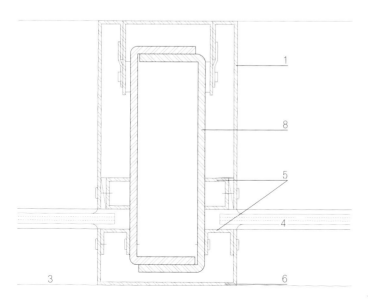

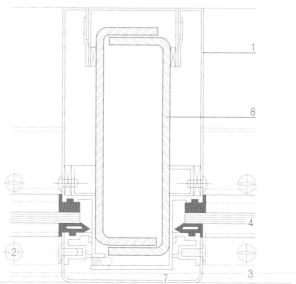

View into the lobby from the street. As part of the project, a new typeface, Lever Sans, was developed from the original building signage.

View of Lever House from the building's third-floor terrace.

◁ Typical plan detail of an original mullion.
Typical plan detail of a new mullion. As a result of the renovation, the facade assembly moved out by a quarter-inch.
1 Original interior closures
2 Stainless-steel fasteners
3 Original face of system
4 Vision glass (removed and replaced)
5 Original carbon-steel glazing stops (removed)
6 Original stainless-steel mullion caps (removed)
7 New stainless-steel mullion caps
8 Original steel mullions (retained)

Ben Gurion International Airport
Tel Aviv, Israel, 2002

This new international terminal complex substantially upgrades the existing facilities at Ben Gurion Airport, creating a modern, spacious environment inspired by Israel's rich history and physical setting. SOM, with Karmi Architects and Lissar Eldar Architects, was commissioned by the Israel Airports Authority to develop design concepts and material standards for the landside and airside terminals as well as the accompanying infrastructure, ranging from approach roads to parking to a train station. The complex, one of the largest building projects that the Israeli government had ever undertaken, was divided into two segments: the landside terminal, designed by SOM, and the airside terminal, designed by Moshe Safdie and Associates. The seven-hundred-thousand-square-foot landside facility includes ticketing, reception, and departures areas; an arrivals complex with a greeters hall; areas for customs and claims; and a stone-clad passport pavilion that symbolizes the gateway to Israel. A two-hundred-meter pedestrian walkway connects the landside terminal to the airside terminal.

The design of the building draws upon Israel's climate and natural resources. The terminal is set in a terraced garden planted with local flora, and its modern palette of metal and glass is juxtaposed with rough-hewn local stone that reflects the natural light entering every large public space. A three-level roadway provides separate access for arriving and departing travelers; a clear glass wall allows views into the building from the roadway. A central "great wall" divides the building: on the lower level it separates the greeters hall from the baggage claim and on the upper level the ticketing hall from the departures hall. The massive wall, clad like the exterior in pale Jerusalem stone, bounces light from skylights above.

Site plan.
1 Landside terminal
2 Airside terminal
3 Garden
4 Parking

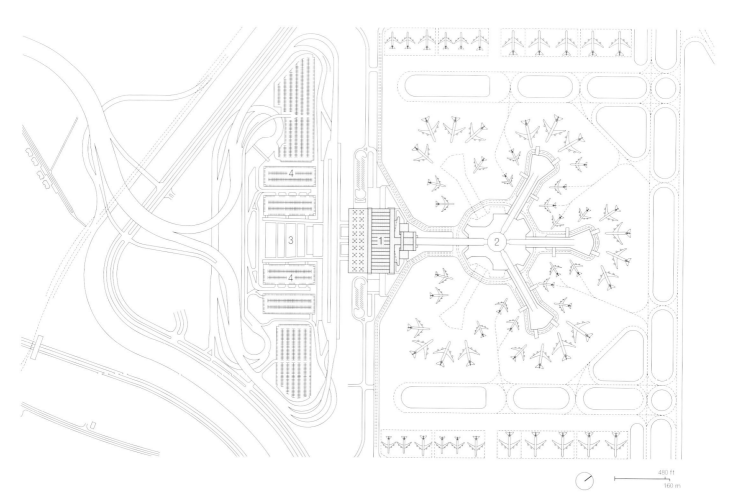

480 ft
160 m

View of the arrivals hall from the mezzanine level.

The landside arrivals level with train station below and roadways to the right.

View of the landside departures hall.

Sections. ▷
1 Ticketing
2 Greeters hall
3 Great wall
4 Departures hall
5 Baggage claim/Arrivals hall
6 Passport control pavilion
7 Train station
8 Roadways
9 Walkways to parking

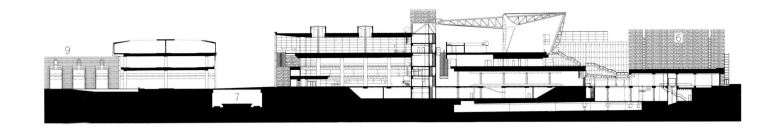

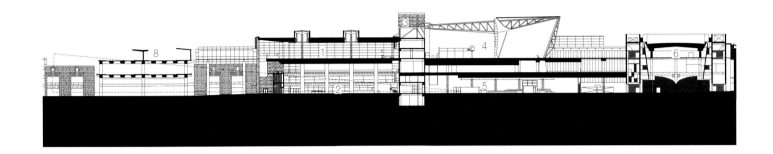

Plan, lower level/arrivals.
Plan, upper level/departures.
1 Greeters hall
2 Customs
3 Baggage claim/Arrivals hall
4 Passport pavilion
5 Departures hall
6 Retail
7 Ticketing hall
8 Immigration
9 Great wall

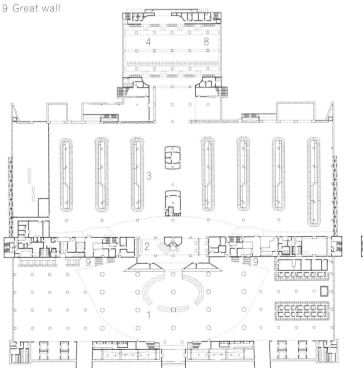

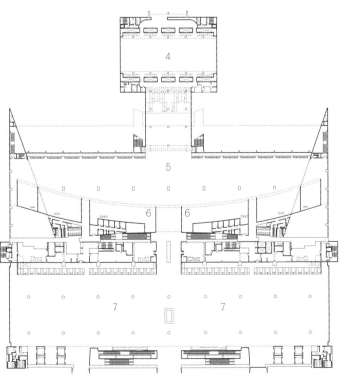

120 ft
40 m

◁ Exterior view of the metal-and-glass window wall and exterior supporting structure of landside terminal.

View from departures hall through the north-facing window wall to activity on the airfield.

View of the great wall. The twenty-seven-foot-deep Jerusalem stone wall reflects sunlight and contrasts with the steel and glass used in the rest of the terminal.

Greenwich Academy Upper School
Greenwich, Connecticut, 2002

The forty-five-thousand-square-foot Greenwich Academy Upper School weaves together the upper and lower levels of the campus and expresses the educational overlap of the school's four academic pillars: science, math, arts and humanities, and the library. The three-story building has a glazed curtain wall supported by laminated exposed timber and a lightweight green roof that maximizes energy efficiency and minimizes groundwater runoff. The roof is perforated by four glass-and-timber light chambers that provide natural light for each of the academic pillars.

The chambers, designed in collaboration with artist James Turrell, connect the school's academic pillars through a common architectural language and create a learning environment infused with daylight and views of nature. This fluidity of building and landscape is further expressed in the interior environment: walls are movable partitions that can expand and contract over time, and furniture on wheels may be arranged in multiple configurations. At night the chambers appear as sculptural volumes defined by the programmable lights integrated into the structure.

Site plan.
1 Upper School
2 Middle School
3 Lower School
4 Cafeteria
5 Assembly hall
6 Campbell Hall
7 Performing arts center
8 Athletic center
9 Athletic fields
10 Entry drive
11 Lake

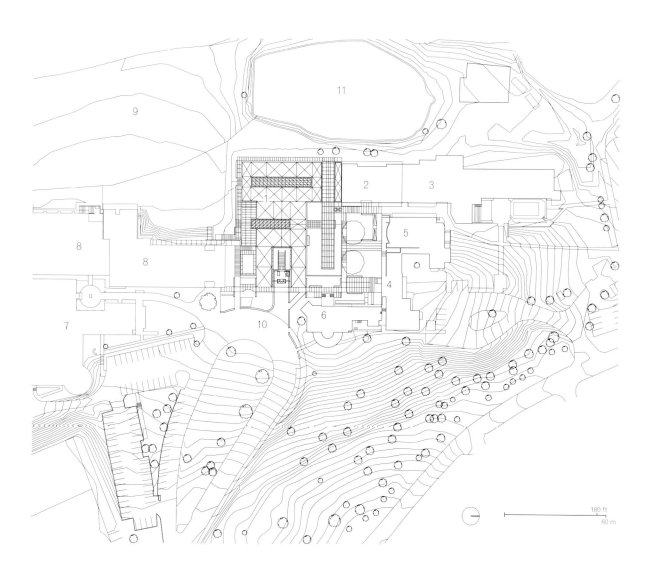

180 ft
60 m

View of the entry/science light chamber from the entry drive. The warm, textural timber elements contrast with the glass. The stone walls were built from rock excavated on the site.

Aerial view of the campus from the southwest.
Four light chambers rise through the landscaped
roof of the Upper School.

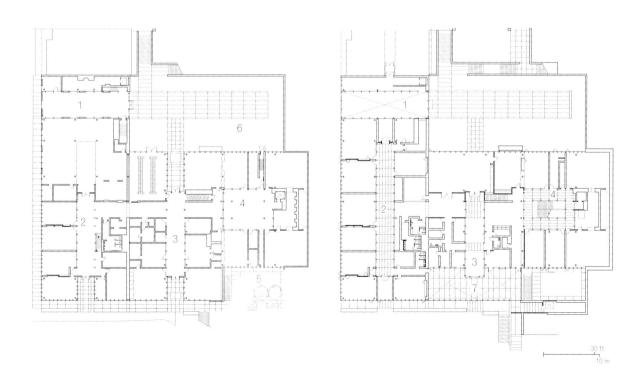

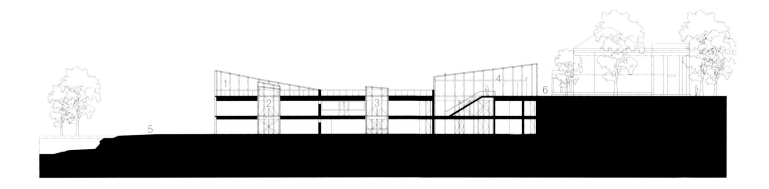

Section. The building negotiates a twenty-three-foot grade change.
1 Learning Center light chamber
2 Humanities light chamber
3 Art light chamber
4 Math and science light chamber/entrance
5 Level of athletic fields/lake
6 Level of upper campus

View from the athletic fields.

Roof-level view of the art light chamber, with the math and science light chamber beyond.

◁ Plan, first/field level.
  Plan, second/terrace level.
  1 Learning Center light chamber
  2 Humanities light chamber
  3 Art light chamber
  4 Math and science light chamber/entrance
  5 Science courtyard
  6 Library courtyard
  7 Terrace

View past science courtyard to light chambers ▷
and green roof.

Four views of entry/science light chamber. The
lighting scheme, a collaboration with artist
James Turrell, uses both fiber optics and LEDs
to produce mutable colors.

Learning center/library.

Typical light chamber ceiling purlin detail.

1 Glazing
2 Glue-laminated wood purlin
3 LED luminaire
4 Cove bracket
5 Power and data connector
6 3 ½" x 2" lighting cavity
7 ¼" opal acrylic lens
8 ½" thru bolt

Glazing details.

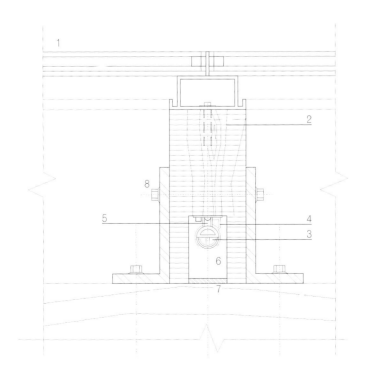

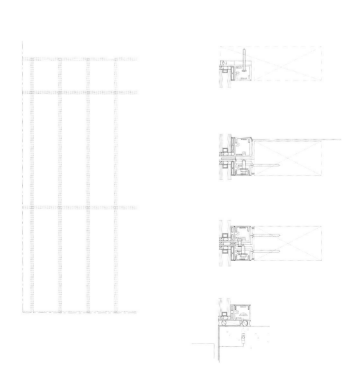

Millennium Park Master Plan
Chicago, Illinois, 2002

This master plan creates a seventeen-acre park, filling a void at the corner of Grant Park and connecting it to Michigan Avenue, with a great lawn, pedestrian bridge, and concert pavilion, providing abundant and varied public space that fulfills Chicago's motto: *Urbs in horto*, or city in a garden. With space for performance, athletics, and public art, like Anish Kapoor's *Cloud Gate* and Jaume Plensa's Crown Fountain, Millennium Park is a key element in an extensive urban revitalization.

The site was most recently a surface parking lot and, before that, a rail freight yard. Similar functions still exist in an underground complex: the park acts as a giant green roof for a multimodal transit center that includes rail lines, bus lanes, large commuter bicycle parking facility, and two-level parking garage.

Two of the major components of the park were designed by Frank O. Gehry Associates and engineered by SOM: an outdoor concert pavilion with a band shell and a pedestrian bridge. The roof of the band shell consists of structural steel cantilevering forty meters from the proscenium arch on the stage. The arch supports a set of organic metal shapes framed with a three-dimensional steel grille. The concert pavilion is comprised of exposed, arched steel members that create an open trellis over the lawn and seating area. The 945-foot-long curving pedestrian bridge, clad in brushed stainless-steel panels, connects the park to a pathway along Lake Michigan, restoring historic connections between the streetscape and the waterway.

Site plan.
1 Exelon Pavilion
2 Harris Theater for Music and Dance
3 Bike station
4 Jay Pritzker Pavilion
5 BP Bridge
6 Lurie Garden
7 Chase Promenade
8 Boeing Gallery
9 Crown Fountain
10 McCormick Tribune Plaza and Ice Rink
11 AT&T Plaza/*Cloud Gate*
12 Wrigley Square and Millennium Park Monument

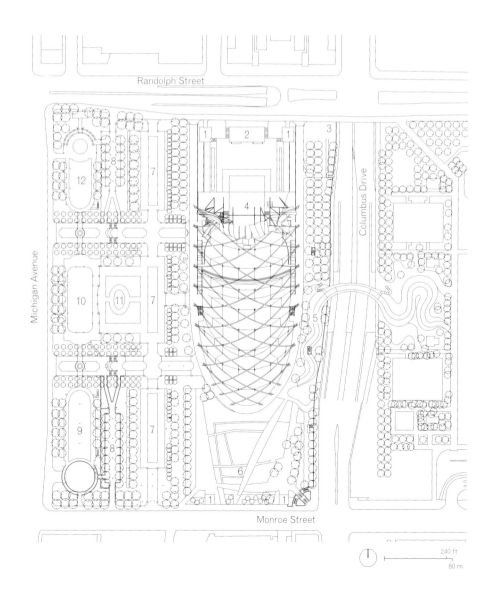

240 ft
80 m

Aerial view from the southeast. The park, which
provides seventeen acres of green space, sits
above an extensive multiuse complex.

AT&T Plaza and Anish Kapoor's *Cloud Gate*.

View from the great lawn to the Jay Pritzker Pavilion. SOM was the structural engineer for this element and for the pedestrian bridge, all of which were designed by Frank O. Gehry Associates.

Lurie Garden.

Detail of BP Bridge.

Crown Fountain, designed by Jaume Plensa with Krueck & Sexton.

Archival view of the site from the northeast. The area was originally a freight rail yard.

UBS AG Center
Stamford, Connecticut, 2002

Located on one of Stamford, Connecticut's last remaining sites along the I-95 corridor, the UBS AG Center is a distinguished group of buildings that serves as the southern gateway to the city. The twelve-acre master plan for the campus will be developed in four phases; the first two phases are complete and provide 1.4 million square feet of space, including offices, trading areas, parking, and indoor and outdoor amenities for private and public use. The main entrance to the complex, along Washington Boulevard, is set into a large landscaped park. SOM integrated the complex into the fabric of the city, rather than aligning it with the highway, and made it and its surroundings more pedestrian-friendly by reinforcing both the urban grid and the view corridors to the Long Island Sound.

At the heart of the campus, on top of a parking podium, sits the largest column-free trading floor in the world. Twelve hundred traders are accommodated in an arching arena 30 to 50 feet high and spanned by 150-foot-long king-post trusses that incorporate a north-facing clerestory window. The truss is lifted to introduce controlled natural light into the trading floor, eliminating glare and connecting the traders with the outdoors. A series of curved baffles, designed to act as reflectors, balances the natural light and provides a complementary indirect light source. These large baffles, which recall puffy clouds, also provide acoustical attenuation for the large open volume below. Additionally, the ceiling design, through the incorporation of a large air-distribution element at the center of each structural bay, seamlessly integrates the environmental controls for the space. The gently curved form of the roof recurs throughout the project, most visibly in the bowed glass facade of the office tower's top, connecting the entire project with the gracious sailboats in the distance.

The front entrance. ▷

Site plan.
1 Trading pavilion
2 Office tower
3 Plaza
4 Parking
5 Interstate 95

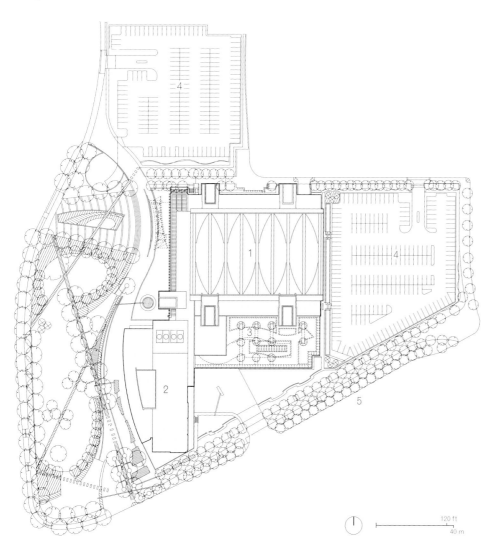

120 ft
40 m

View of the west facade of the trading pavilion and the office tower.

Section.
1 Trading floor
2 Data center
3 Parking
4 Entry terrace
5 Ramp

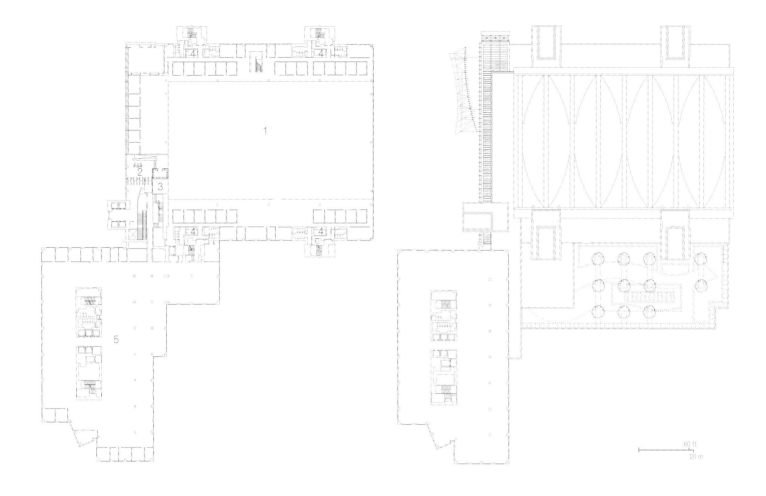

Plan, sixth floor.
1 Trading floor
2 Lobby
3 Conference area
4 Kitchen
5 Trading support and offices

Plan, typical tower floor.

Interior view looking toward the reception area.

View of the trading floor and its fluid suspended ceiling.

Entry to the Center for Learning and Development.

View from an executive office looking out over the trading floor.

Logan International Airport: International Gateway Project, Terminal E
Boston, Massachusetts, 2003

As part of Logan International Airport's $1 billion modernization program, International Terminal E has been renovated and expanded both to double its capacity and to forge a connection to the city. A multilevel addition designed by SOM includes a new ticketing hall, larger retail facilities, and dual-level roadway system.

The primary design feature is a glass curtain wall facing out to Boston Harbor and the city skyline: arriving and departing passengers are presented with panoramic views of the city of Boston. Five three-story, free-standing glass vestibules bridge the roadway and the building. At night, these vestibules become lanterns, visible from downtown Boston. Inside, transition points are marked by architectural elements that incorporate light. A warm material palette complements the wooden wall and ceiling panels. Backlit wood-and-glass walls divide the ticketing and retail areas, as well as security and the gate concourse. Fritted-glass light columns also recur throughout the terminal: between customs and the arrivals hall, between retail and security, and framing the elevators and stairs near the departures roadway.

Site plan.
1 Existing terminal
2 Terminal Expansion
3 Dual-level roadway

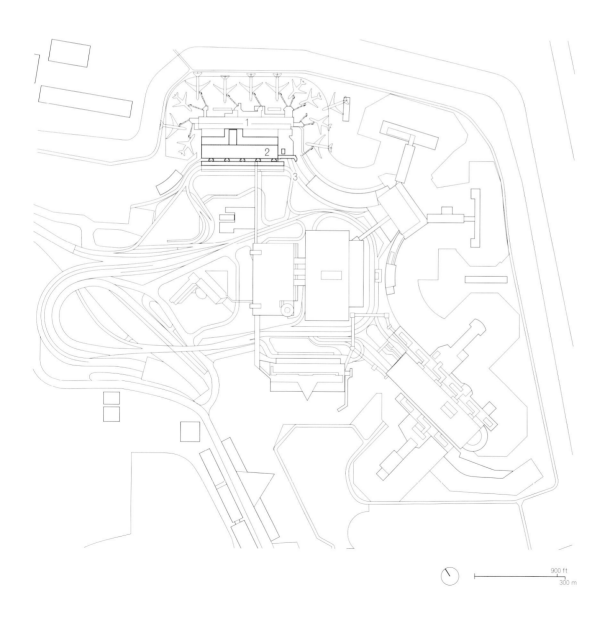

900 ft
300 m

The departures hall. Steamed-beech ceiling
panels complement the wood-and-glass wall
above the ticket counters.

Plan, first floor/arrivals area.

1 Arrivals roadway
2 Arrivals hall
3 International baggage claim
4 Domestic baggage claim
5 Taxi pickup

Plan, second floor/departures area.

1 Upper-level roadway
2 Departures curb
3 Check-in hall
4 Retail
5 Security
6 Gate lounges
7 Airline offices
8 Walkway to concourse D

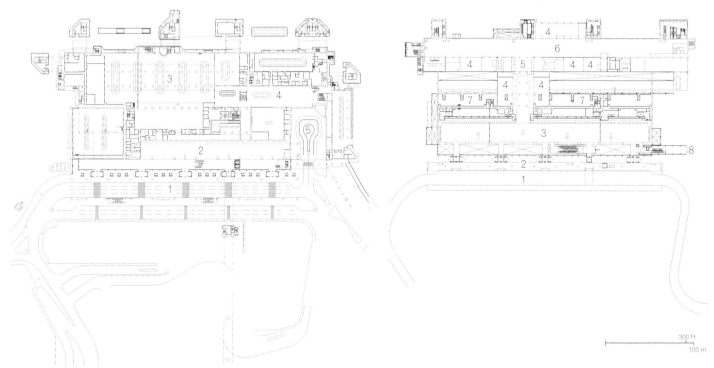

300 ft
100 m

◁ View from the street into the terminal, with the departures hall above and the arrivals hall below. One of the five fritted-glass vestibules, or lanterns, is in the foreground on the right.

View of the backlit wall above the ticket counters in the departures hall. The wall is made of Douglas fir veneer and glass.

The departures hall. The predominantly warm palette of materials, with wood panels on the walls and ceilings, contrasts with the stainless-steel ticket counters.

Day and night views of the lanterns. The crystalline forms are visible through the glass curtain wall.

Section.
1 Check-in hall
2 Retail hall
3 Gate lounge
4 Arrivals hall
5 Immigration
6 International baggage claim
7 Mechanical
8 Lantern

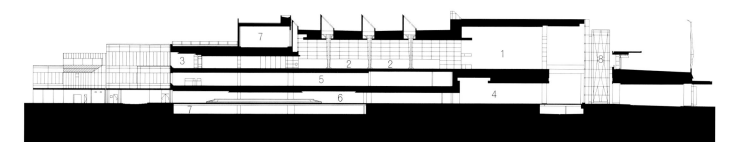

View from a second-floor bridge to one of the lanterns.

View of a lantern. Each of the five vestibules is unique, using the same components in a different configuration.

Burr Street Elementary School
Fairfield, Connecticut, 2004

This Fairfield County elementary school shares an unusually close relationship with its wooded fifteen-acre site. The seventy-one-thousand-square-foot building is square in plan, with voids carved out to accommodate existing trees and form indoor landscaped courtyards with glazed walls.

The two-story building is organized so that the classrooms are at the east and west perimeter walls and the shared areas are at the center. Two cutouts form entry courts, with drop-off areas for parents and school buses. These separate routes eliminate the need for a perimeter road and allow each classroom to have a direct view of the wooded landscape. Four internal voids flood the communal spaces—corridors, library, music area—with daylight. The cutouts also inform the organization of the interior spaces, dividing certain areas into "bubbles" for different functions and creating both visual connectivity and acoustic separation.

Full-height glazing at the east and west facades allows maximum daylighting. The north and south facades are more opaque and have a high R value to mitigate heat gain and loss. The site was graded to minimize disturbance to the existing topography, and a bank of holding ponds with cattails and other indigenous plants retains storm water, filtering and then releasing it to an adjacent wetland.

Site plan.
1 Burr Street Elementary School
2 Parent drop-off
3 Bus drop-off
4 Parking
5 Wetlands
6 Athletic field
7 Burr Street

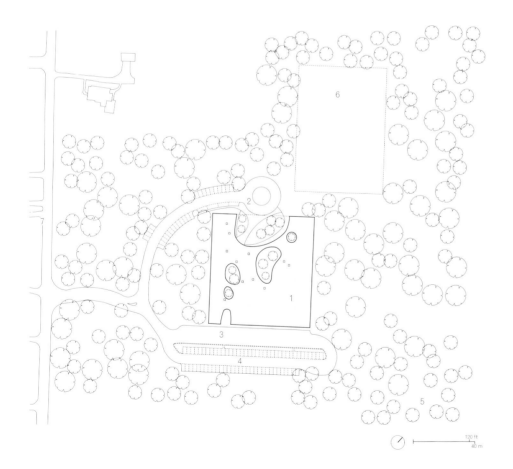

Aerial view from the north. The school, set in a heavily wooded area, accommodates existing trees in its plan.

Parent drop-off.

Section through the library. ▷
 1 Kindergarten
 2 Second grade
 3 Corridor
 4 Library/Media center
 5 Courtyard B
 6 Music room
 7 Special education
 8 Courtyard C
 9 Fourth grade
10 Speech

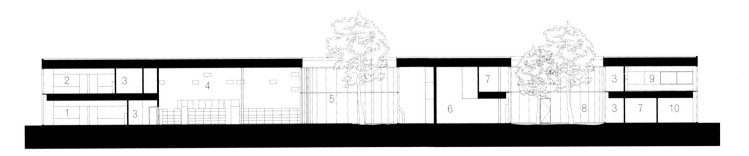

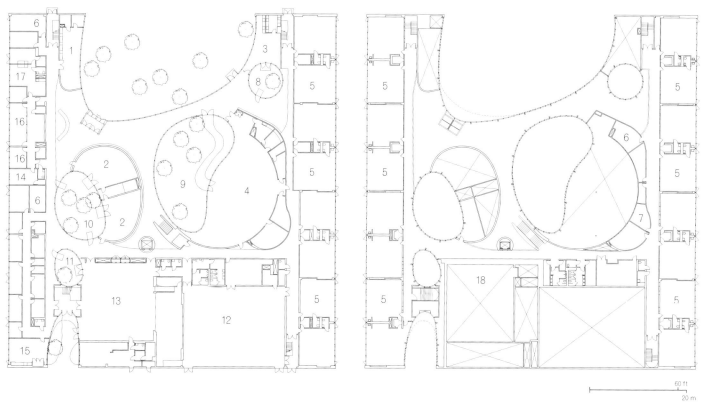

◁ View of the library courtyard, with library on the right and main entry courtyard behind the curved glass wall on the left.

View of an interior courtyard.

View of a hallway formed by two interior courtyards.

◁ Plan, first floor.
Plan, second floor.
 1 Art
 2 Music
 3 Science
 4 Library/Media center
 5 Classroom
 6 Special education
 7 Gifted math
 8 Courtyard A
 9 Courtyard B
 10 Courtyard C
 11 Courtyard D
 12 Gymnasium/Auditorium
 13 Cafeteria
 14 Principal's office
 15 Faculty lunch
 16 Conference room
 17 Nurse's station
18 Mechanical

Chongming Island Master Plan
Shanghai, China, 2004

Long considered Shanghai's "rice bowl," Chongming Island is one of the largest alluvial islands in the world—750 square miles—and is recognized for its rich and fertile land. Located at the mouth of the Yangtze River, the island is home to more than six hundred thousand people and operates as one of Shanghai's five municipal districts.

The new master plan bridges the ecological and the urban. It repositions Chongming as a "green island," promoting agricultural output and preserving the natural wetlands that serve Asia's primary avian flyways. The scheme embraces Shanghai's rapid growth by developing eight new cities—for a population of nearly a million people—that are walkable, accessible, connected, and cover only 15 percent of the island. The master plan centers on eight themes: habitat enhancement, organic farming, sustainable industries, transportation, village preservation, coastal cities, green infrastructure, and wilderness protection. Each of these themes is addressed through a combination of planning, agriculture, and architecture.

As part of the design process, a team specializing in organic farming, hydrology, and sustainability approached the problems inherent in island agriculture—such as seawater leaking into underground aquifers—and suggested ecologically friendly solutions. One such strategy is a chain of lakes that runs down the spine of the island and operates as a series of gray-water biofilters. The lakes are linked to a canal system that feeds carefully selected high-profit crops. Those, in turn, are supplied to farmers' markets, upscale food stores, and restaurants, continuing the sophisticated web of connections.

Site plan. ▷
1 Chongming Island
2 Qidong
3 East China Sea
4 Mouth of the Yangtze River
5 Pudong Airport
6 Shanghai
7 Huang Pu River

Aerial view of Chongming Island, showing its proximity to the city of Shanghai to the south and to the China Sea to the east.

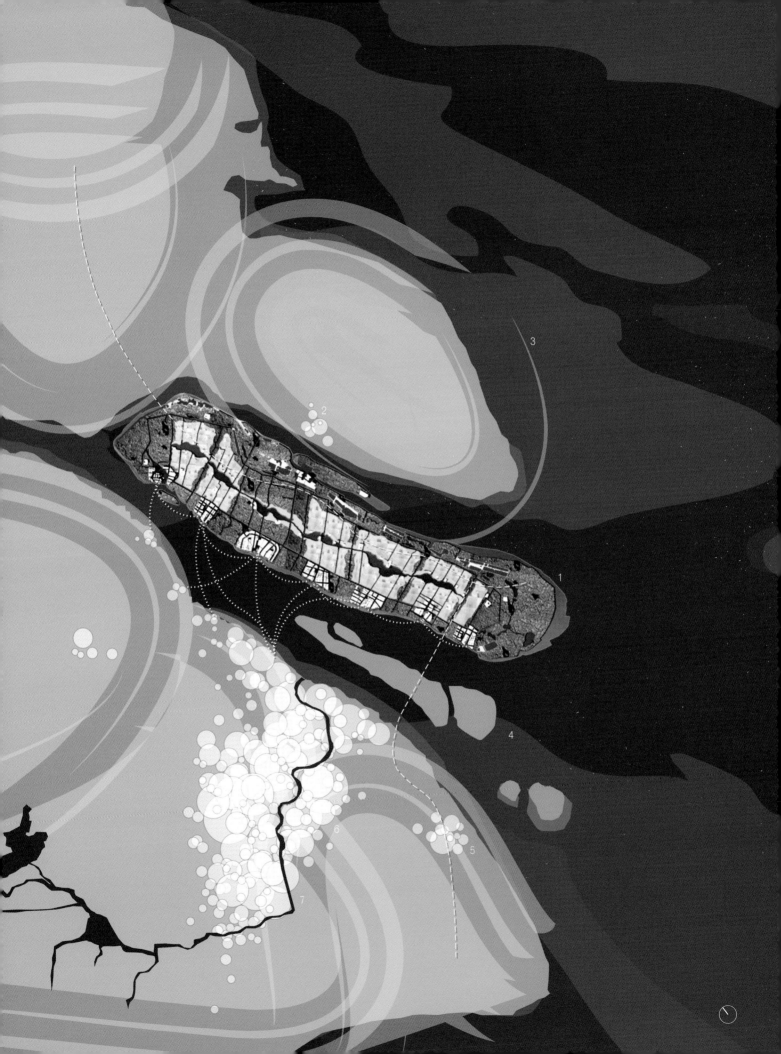

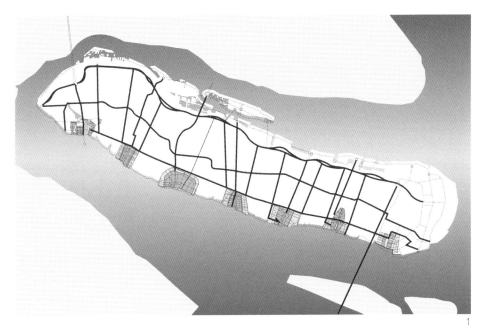

Plans showing the main planning and urban design concepts.
1 Red lines: preservation of historic narrow street grid
2 Red circles: forty farm villages (200,000 residents)
3 Light green: rural/agricultural areas (35 percent of the island)
4 Blue waterway: six lakes
5 Red/orange grids: eight cities (600,000 residents) with rail connections to Shanghai
6 Dark green: protected wilderness areas (55 percent of the island)

1

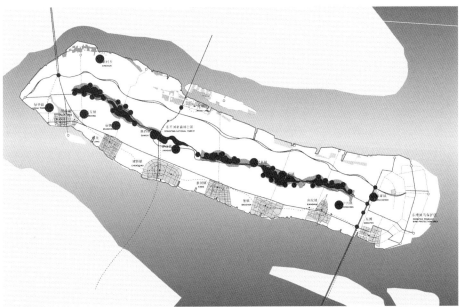

2

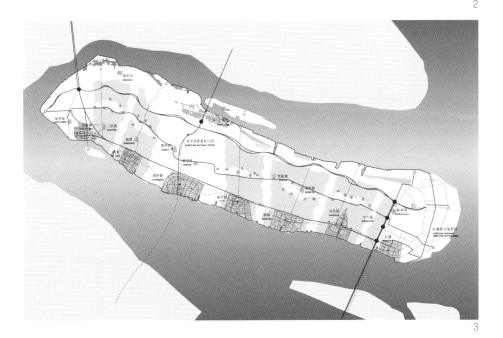

3

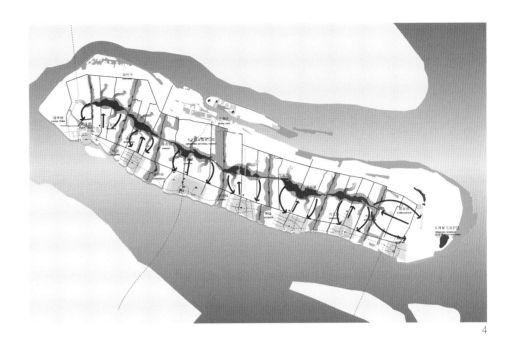

4

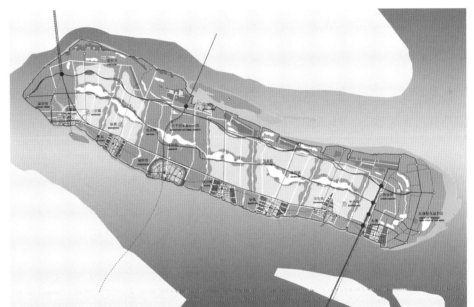

5

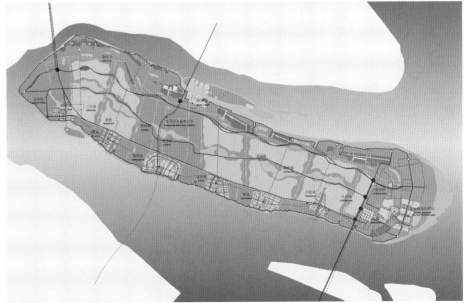

6

Lenovo/Raycom Infotech Park: Building C
Beijing, China, 2004

The campus of Lenovo/Raycom Infotech Park is defined not only by workplace efficiency and technological innovation but also by a lush gardenlike setting removed from the surrounding urbanized business district in Beijing. Lenovo/Raycom Building C, a ninety-thousand-square-meter complex consisting of two seventeen-story towers with a glass-walled pavilion between them, is SOM's second project for the company.

A double-wall system protects the interiors from the harsh Beijing weather and provides sun screening, while the shape of the towers—the long facades run east-west, the short ones north-south—maximizes efficient daylight and minimizes sun glare. The space between the west exterior screen walls and the inner glass walls is open at the top and bottom to create a fully ventilated cavity. The finely textured south walls have horizontal glass fins suspended from cantilevered grilles by stainless-steel rods.

The column-free pavilion, which acts like a bridge, is comprised of a structural cable-net wall and roof system. The roof, designed to withstand seismic activity, is suspended between the flanking office towers. At each attachment point are four stainless-steel connectors; two are fixed and two are flexible, fitting into slots with spherical rotating receivers. The glass pavilion provides entry to the towers and also to the below-grade retail and conference spaces; within are four specially commissioned artworks. Bamboo grows upward from the lower level to the entrance and gathering spaces.

View of the entry pavilion and north tower. ▷

Site plan.
1 Building A
2 Building C
3 Drop-off and main entry
4 Retail
5 Court
6 Garden

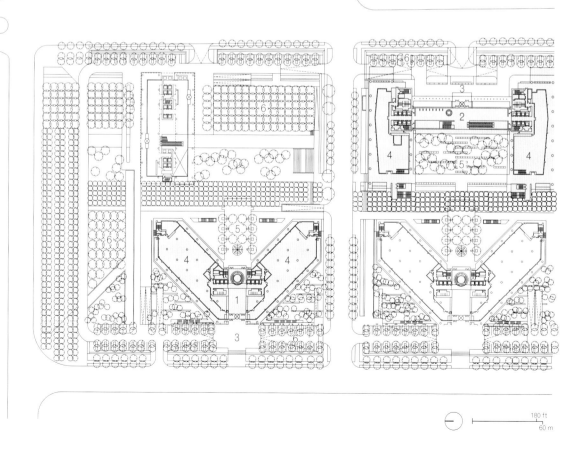

180 ft
60 m

The glass pavilion. This structure has a seventy-five-meter-long cable-net wall and serves as a bridge between the two office towers.

View through the glass pavilion to the gardens beyond.

View from the pavilion to the exterior court.

◁ View of the southwest corner of the south office tower. On the south facade, seen at the right, a glass screen wall shields the double-glazed enclosure.

Typical section through south office tower facade.
1 Fritted laminated horizontal glass fins
2 Metal grate catwalk
3 Operable window
4 Summer sun angle
5 Spring/fall sun angle
6 Winter sun angle
7 Exposed concrete structure
8 Mechanical plenum
9 Raised floor for power and data

View down the length of the entry pavilion. The glass extends below ground level and into the reflecting pool.

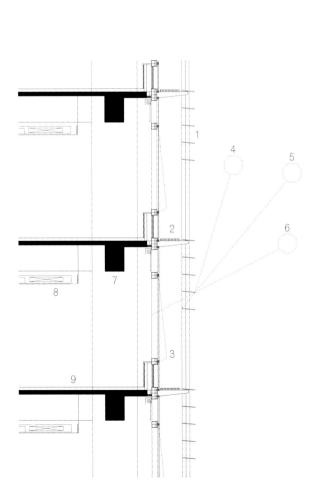

View from northwest. The narrow east and west facades maximize daylight yet reduce solar gain.

Artworks by Sui Jianguo, which were commissioned for the pavilion.

Section.
1 Typical office
2 Elevator lobby bay window
3 Entry pavilion
4 Lower-level retail and restaurants
5 Parking
6 Retail

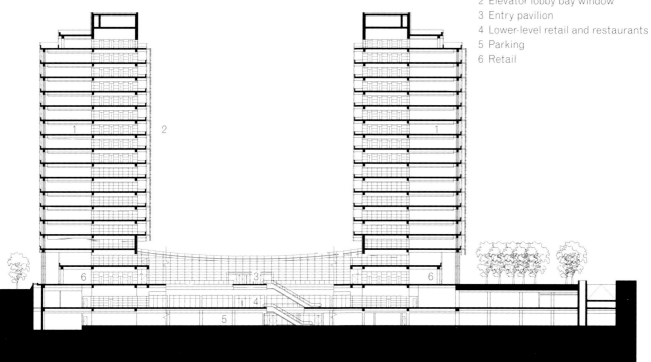

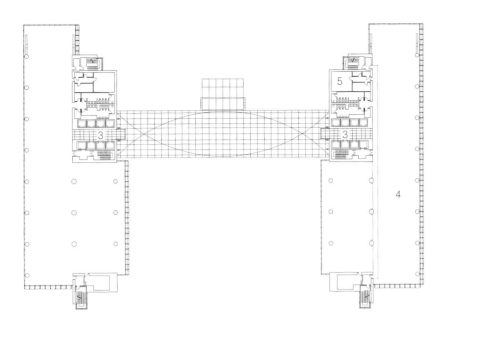

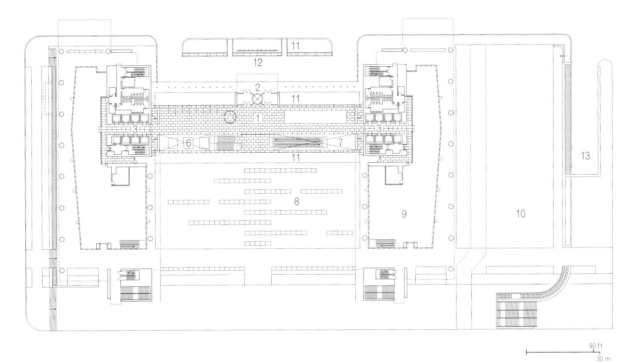

Plan, typical office level.
Plan, ground level.
 1 Entry pavilion
 2 Canopy and vestibule
 3 Elevator lobby
 4 Typical office
 5 Mechanical space
 6 Bamboo planters at lower level
 7 Escalators to lower-level retail
 8 Court with skylights to lower level
 9 Retail
10 Garden
11 Water feature
12 Drop-off and entry
13 Ramp to parking

Skyscraper Museum
New York, New York, 2004

The Skyscraper Museum conveys the grandeur of the skyscraper, even in its limited quarters, through attention to materials, sightlines, and details. Located on the first floor of the Battery Park Ritz-Carlton, the museum occupies five thousand square feet of donated space. The floors and ceilings are finished with perfectly flat, polished stainless-steel panels. Undistorted reflections maximize the apparent volume of the exhibition space, making it seem to extend endlessly in the vertical direction. Together with tall, internally illuminated exhibit vitrines, which allow the galleries to be reconfigured for different exhibitions and events, the reflective surfaces create an environment that alludes to the idea of the skyscraper itself. A series of ramps connects the bookstore and entrance areas at sidewalk level to the main gallery level and to the administration and workroom areas.

View of the gallery. The mirror-finish stainless-steel panels on the floor and ceiling make the space seem taller than its actual height. ▷

◁ View up the entrance ramp at the ground floor with the bookstore at the right.

View of the movable display volumes in the gallery space.

Plan, ground floor.
Plan, mezzanine.
1 Entrance
2 Ramp
3 Bookstore
4 Gallery
5 Restrooms
6 Offices

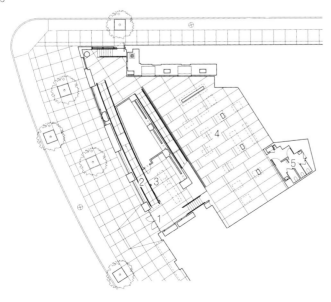

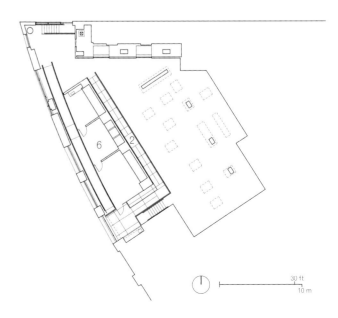

Time Warner Center
New York, New York, 2004

Because of its extraordinarily complex program, the Time Warner Center, perhaps to a greater degree than any other modern American building, exemplifies the concept of a city within a building, rather than a building within a city. In addition to service, transit, and parking infrastructure, the mixed-use project encompasses the corporate headquarters of Time Warner, including production facilities for CNN and other Time Warner media outlets; the Shops at Columbus Circle, a retail and restaurant complex; Jazz at Lincoln Center, a multihall performance and education facility; the five-star Mandarin Oriental Hotel; a large health club; and the One Central Park luxury condominiums.

This multifaceted program presented numerous challenges. SOM addressed issues of structure, stacking, vertical circulation, and mechanical systems, as well as New York City's guidelines for this site. For example, two different structural systems were necessary: steel for the podium, to maintain the clear spans required by the broadcast, office, and hotel ballroom areas, and a truss-transfer system to concrete superstructure above, as is typical for residential and hotel construction. In addition, each of the major building elements required its own vertical circulation, which had to be inserted into the building in a way that would not disrupt the column-free spaces mandated by each of the tenants.

The building's five-story, granite-clad retail podium is punctuated by large glass openings, including a 150-foot-tall cable-net glass wall that serves as the building's main entrance. As the building ascends to the midrise studios and offices, the masonry dissolves into a glassy skin. The two glass towers above culminate in illuminated crowns.

The simplicity of the building's form belies the complexity within even as it responds to the essence of the urban context from which it emanates. The main entrance to the complex is on axis with Fifty-ninth Street, figuratively reestablishing the missing portion of this major artery. The separation between the two towers establishes an eighty-five-foot-wide view corridor beginning 185 feet above grade. The curved facade follows the arc of Columbus Circle, establishing a relationship between the site and the public realm outside. Along with the use of setbacks, these formal decisions both minimize the impact of the 2.8-million-square-foot project and maximize its role as a fulcrum connecting the West Side, Midtown, and Central Park.

View from the southeast. The massing of ▷ the building responds to the vectors of the prominent site: the curve of Columbus Circle, the city grid, and the angle of Broadway.

Plan, ground floor with site context.
 1 Time Warner entrance
 2 Residential entrance
 3 Retail entrance
 4 Subway entrance
 5 Jazz/retail entrance
 6 Office entrance
 7 Hotel/residential lobby
 8 Retail
 9 Jazz
10 Loading
11 Ramp to parking

Eighth Avenue

58th Street

60th Street

Broadway

Central Park West

Broadway

Central Park South

60 ft
20 m

View of the residential entrance.

View of the performance space for Jazz at Lincoln Center. With the musicians set in front of the cable-net wall, the city becomes a backdrop for the stage.

View from the atrium toward Columbus Circle. The glass cable-net wall is 150 feet tall.

Exterior view of the cable-net wall.

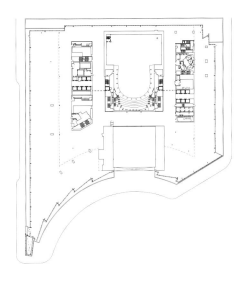 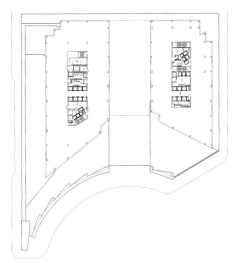 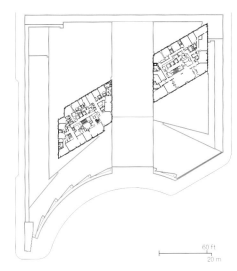

Plan, Time Warner floor.

Plan, typical office floor.

Plan, typical residential floor.

Night view along Fifty-eighth Street. The shape of the towers continues the diagonal line of Broadway.

◁ The main retail entrance.

Atrium.

View of the steel-framed glass prow. At night, it is illuminated by an LED sculpture that changes color every three minutes.

Cable-net detail.
1 Exterior elevation
2 Interior elevation
3 Section

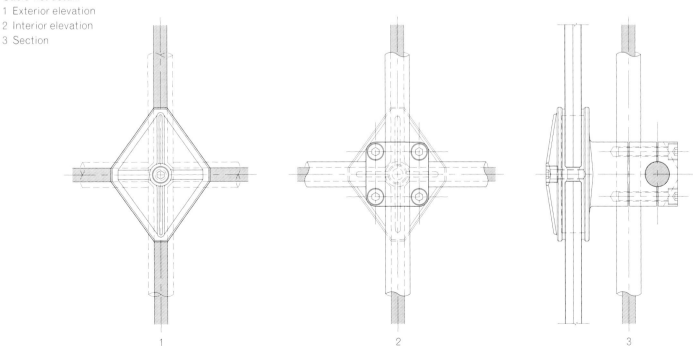

1

2

3

View of the Manhattan skyline from the west. The
Time Warner Center's towers are at the far left.

View from Central Park. The void between the
towers expresses the axis of the street.

Section.
1 Columbus Circle
2 Time Warner
3 Cable-net wall
4 Atrium
5 Whole Foods
6 Health club
7 Retail
8 Loading
9 Parking
10 Jazz at Lincoln Center performance space
11 Rose Hall auditorium
12 Stage
13 Fly gallery
14 Time Warner boardroom

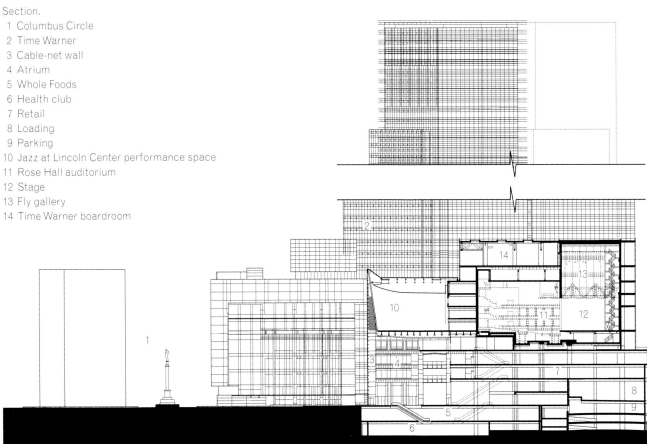

Hyatt Global Headquarters
Chicago, Illinois, 2004

This 280,000-square-foot headquarters, which occupies seven stories in Chicago's Hyatt Center, combines the typology of the modern hotel with that of the modern office. Voids carved out of each floor activate the space and pay homage to Hyatt's innovative concept of the hotel atrium.

The main reception area on the twelfth floor is two stories high, with bronze mesh drapes in front of full-height glazing. Other reception spaces include a library, dining room, and lounge. A grand staircase leads from the reception to the boardroom and other executive facilities, and a stainless steel-and-glass stair connects to the public hospitality spaces on each floor, which are housed in cantilevered wooden volumes.

The interiors use rich materials and colors; clean lines suggest a fusion of East and West. Various interior elements—handrail of the grand stair, reception desk, boardroom table—were crafted of walnut in collaboration with designer Mira Nakashima.

View of the reception area on the twelfth floor. ▷ The grand stair, at the left, is made of walnut, and the staircase that connects the other levels in the atrium is made of blue-green glass.

Plan, twelfth floor.
1 Reception
2 Seating area
3 Library
4 Meeting room
5 Elevator lobby
6 Office
7 Conference room
8 Employee lounge

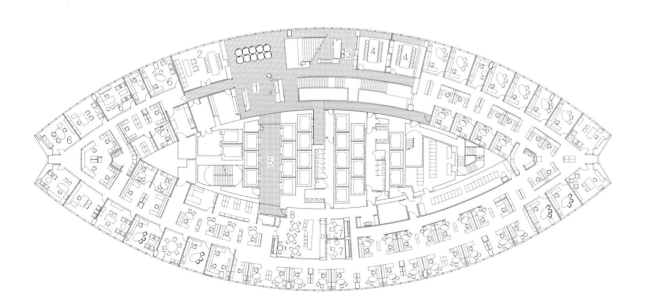

60 ft
20 m

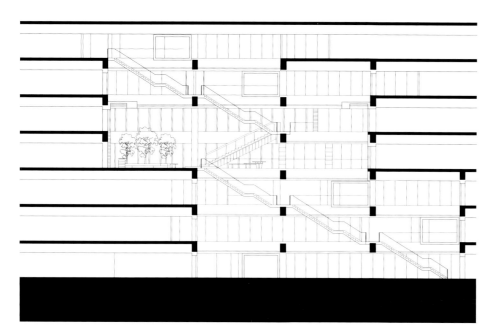

View of the atrium. Walnut-clad volumes ▷
protrude into the space.

Section through the seven-story atrium.

The boardroom.

Jianianhua Center
Chongqing, China, 2005

Built as part of a master redevelopment plan for Chongqing's commercial district Jiangbei, the forty-four-thousand-square-meter Jianianhua Center anchors a new central park and plaza. The mixed-use complex is comprised of a seven-story retail center and a fifteen-story office tower; clad in glass, the buildings contrast with neighboring concrete structures.

Jianianhua Center's prominent feature is a large-scale graphic billboard, a nod to the signs that appear throughout the commercial district. Set within the lower building's double-wall system are three-sided motorized signage panels; these panels rotate at different intervals to create changing images. The panels also form a layer that protects the interior from changes in temperature. The large, monolithic sheets of glass of the outer skin minimize the number of structural mullions and emphasize the signage within. A skylit central atrium provides natural light to the interior retail spaces.

The office tower has a skin of tall, narrow, insulated-glass panels. The proportions of the glazing panels relate to those of the sign panels in the adjacent building, and interior louvers mitigate solar gain.

Site plan of park and commercial district.
1 Jianianhua Center
2 Pedestrian promenade
3 City central plaza
4 Park

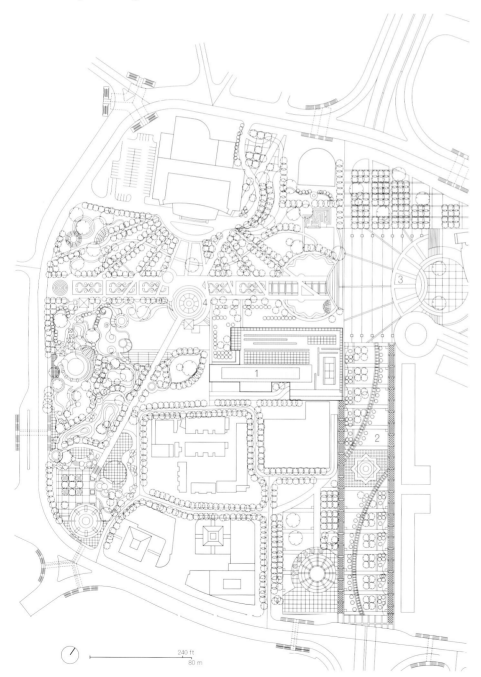

240 ft
80 m

View of Jianianhua Center from the park.

Views of the southwest facade with rotating billboard graphic.

Plan, retail level.

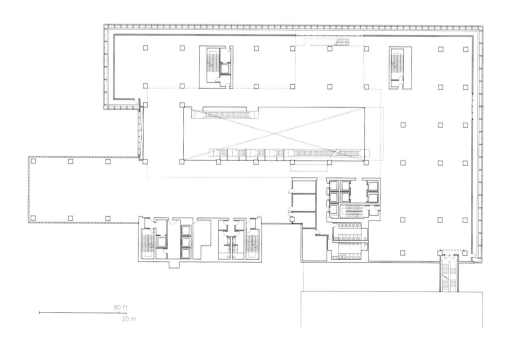

60 ft
20 m

Plan, typical office floor.

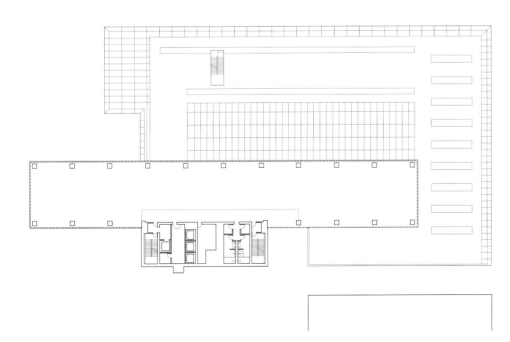

◁ View of the interior with the skylight above and the three-sided signage panels.

View from the west.

Section at graphic wall.
Plan at graphic wall.
1 Glass enclosure
2 Service walkway
3 Rotating sign panel
4 Skylight
5 Wood soffit

Pages 128–129:
View of the large-scale graphic billboard.

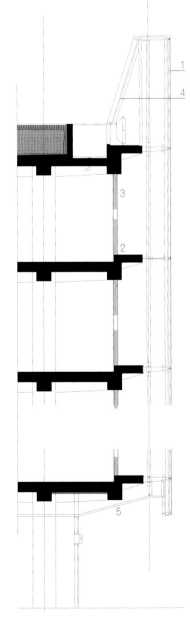

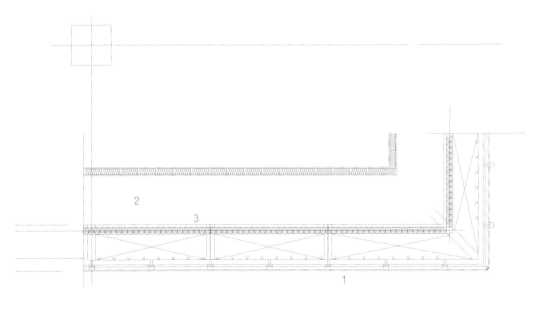

University of California Merced: Central Plant Complex and Information-Technology Center
Merced, California, 2005

The campus of the University of California Merced sits on a two-thousand-acre agricultural site in the San Joaquin Valley, near the foothills of the Sierra Madre Mountains. The master plan envisions a community that will grow to include twenty-five thousand students. A long-term development plan and architectural design guidelines provide a model for sustainable growth within the ecologically significant site. Materials, energy use, and sustainability maintain a high level of resource conservation. The first phase of the master plan includes a library and information-technology center and a central plant complex, each awarded a LEED Gold rating.

The library and information-technology center is prominently located at the end of a pedestrian bridge between dormitories and athletic buildings. It serves as a gateway building for the university and houses a student union, classrooms, and facilities for administration and technology in addition to the library. The L-shaped plan consists of three main components: two wings joined by a central entry space clad in fritted-glass louvers and a four-story lantern that houses the student commons on the first two floors and reading room above. Glazing is set back from the exposed concrete frame, which provides sun shading. Operable roll-up doors, louvers, overhangs, and arcades form spaces that bridge indoors and outdoors, creating an openness for this campus hub. At night, the glowing metal-and-glass lantern is a visual landmark within the campus.

The central plant complex anchors the sustainability-focused infrastructure of the university and is comprised of three elements: three-story plant building, thermal storage tank, and telecom building. The plant building and tank sit on a concrete plinth partially embedded in the sloping site. The plinth helps enclose the telecom service yard. Across the yard is the low telecom building. Industrial cladding applied in an innovative manner creates a striking, prominent image for infrastructural elements that are often disguised. The three-story, forty-one-thousand-square-foot plant building is clad in perforated corrugated stainless steel; a band of channel glass just above the base introduces natural light. The adjacent storage tank, which contains chilled water for the entire campus, has a skin of lightly reflective corrogated-stainless-steel shingles.

Street view of the central plant from the north. ▷
The building is clad in perforated corrugated stainless steel.

Master plan.
1 Central plant
2 Library and information-technology center

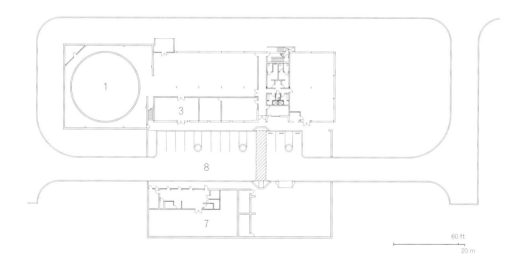

View from the southeast. The thermal storage tank is clad in stainless-steel shingles. Its solidity is a contrast to the perforated steel of the plant building.

Plan, lower level.
Sections.
1 Thermal energy storage tank
2 Chiller pumps
3 Control room
4 Cooling tower
5 Boilers
6 Switchgear
7 Telecommunications equipment and office
8 Service yard
9 Water pump
10 Perforated metal wall for sound reduction
11 Utility tunnel for campus distribution

60 ft
20 m

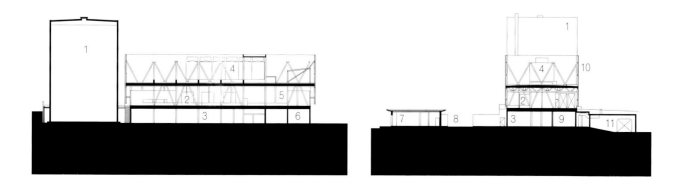

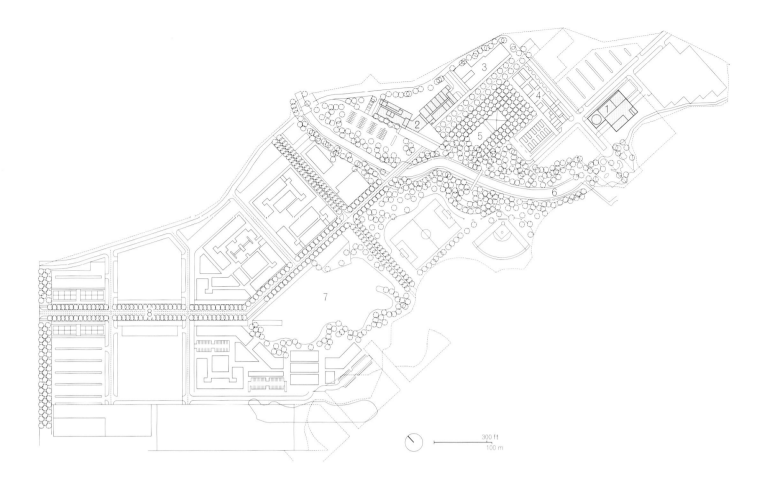

Campus plan, phase one.
1 Central plant
2 Library and information-technology center
3 Classroom building
4 Science building
5 Central green
6 Canal
7 Pond
8 Entry drive

Bridge detail at the thermal energy storage tank.

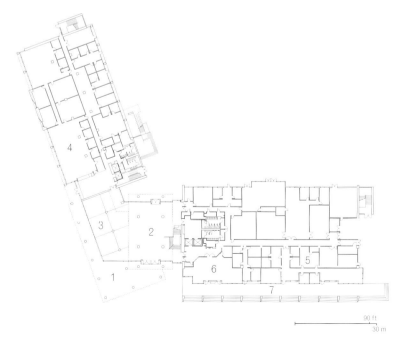

View of the library and information-technology center from the canal.

Plan, first level.
1 Entry loggia
2 Entry/information
3 Campus living room
4 Admission/student services
5 Student clubs
6 Bookstore
7 Arcade

90 ft
30 m

Plan, fourth level.
Plan, third level.
Plan, second level.
1 Library
2 Campus reading room
3 Periodicals reading room
4 Campus administration
5 Classrooms
6 Circulation desk/Library entry

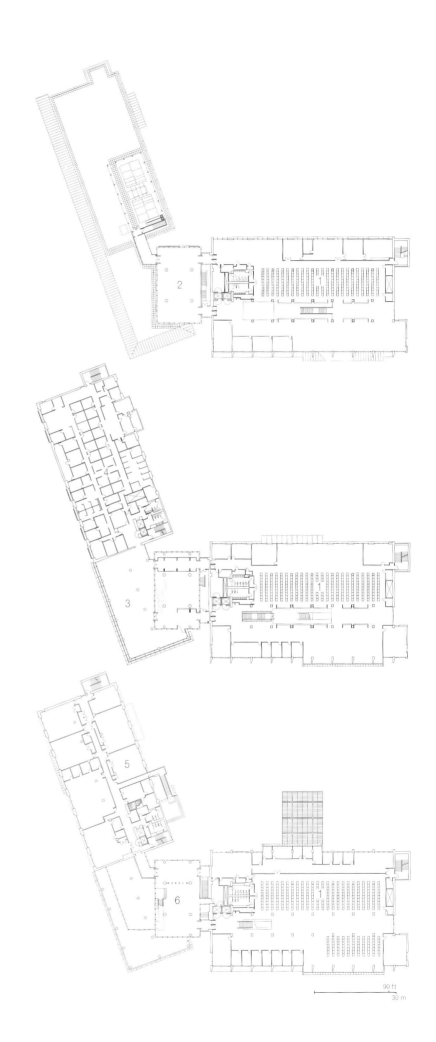

90 ft
30 m

View of the central entry area. The library and information-technology center acts as a nexus for the campus and creates a community space.

View of the campus reading room.

View of the entry loggia.

Section through library.
1 Library
2 Bookstore
3 Student club rooms
4 Campus living room
5 Periodicals reading room
6 Campus reading room
7 Circulation desk
8 Clerestory

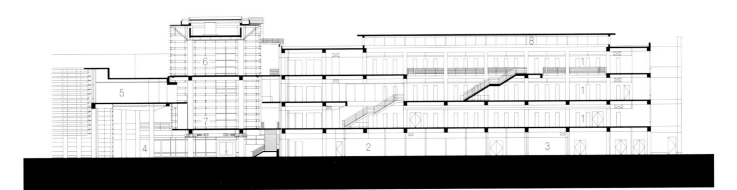

7 World Trade Center
New York, New York, 2006

The new 7 World Trade Center heralds the spirit of redevelopment and renewal in Lower Manhattan after September 11, 2001. The fifty-two-story, 1.7-million-square-foot glass pylon marks the entrance to the World Trade Center and, with its attention to detail and formal restraint, urban planning, clarity of design, life-safety standards, sustainability, and construction quality, establishes a benchmark for future buildings on the site.

Paramount among the urban planning concerns was knitting Tribeca and the Financial District back together. SOM made a convincing case for setting the building back 115 feet from the eastern property line of the parcel in order to extend Greenwich Street southward through the World Trade Center site and reestablish the city grid. The loss of approximately three hundred thousand square feet of rentable area was offset in part by an extension of the site on the south: this side now aligns with adjacent Vesey Street facades. On the triangular plot created by the lengthened Greenwich Street and West Broadway, a new public park provides open space, light, and views.

The original 7 World Trade Center, constructed over a Con Edison substation, placed office space above ten existing transformer vaults and a number of service ramps. With the smaller footprint of the new building, the vaults, which provide much of the power to Lower Manhattan, were reconfigured into an eighty-six-foot-high vertical stack on the north and south sides of the site, forming the tower's podium. The exterior skin of this podium is a dynamic screen that engages the streetscape and accommodates the airflow requirements of the transformers. The highly detailed, stainless-steel wall assembly, designed in collaboration with artist James Carpenter, consists of two rows of vertical triangular steel rods. The double-layer screen creates a moiré effect for pedestrians walking by. On the east facade, a 50-by-110-foot cable-net glass wall set between the rows of transformers marks the building's entrance.

Above the metal-screened podium rises the office tower, which is wrapped in ultra-clear glass. The low-iron glass appears, at times, to dematerialize into the sky. A gradient ceramic frit pattern applied to the upper zone of each glazing panel reduces heat gain without affecting the views or the daylight entering the building. From the interior, the floor-to-ceiling clear-glass units and transparent corners provide a sense of openness and allow for panoramic vistas in all directions. The abundant natural light and interior daylighting controls reduce dependence on artificial lighting. Along with other sustainable design strategies, this approach earned 7 World Trade Center LEED Gold certification, the first high-rise office building in New York City to earn this distinction.

Twilight view from the south. The tower's curtain ▷ wall is both transparent and reflective.

Site plan.
1 World Trade Center site
2 7 World Trade Center
3 World Financial Center

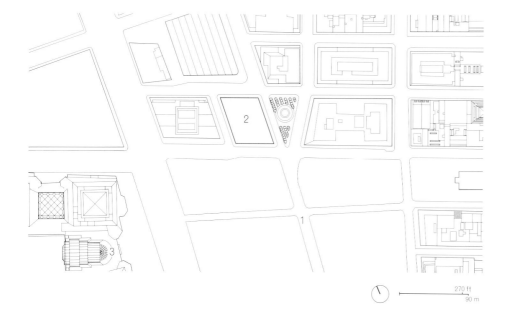

270 ft
90 m

View of entrance lobby. A large LED text installation by artist Jenny Holzer features excerpts of writings on the city's history moving along a protective glass wall.

Plans, ground and typical floors. The tower was pulled back from the property line so that Greenwich Street could extend to Vesey Street, continuing the city grid and creating a new public park.
A 7 World Trade Center
B Park
1 Lobby
2 Elevators
3 Transformer vaults
4 Loading dock

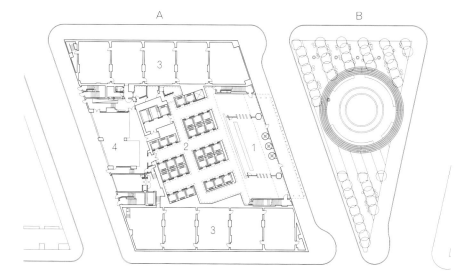

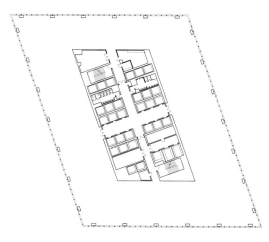

90 ft
30 m

View of the entrance from the new park formed
by extending Greenwich Street. *Balloon Flower
(Red)* is by Jeff Koons.

Section.
1 Lobby
2 Podium
3 Tower

Podium section.
1 Transformer vault
2 Screen wall
3 Control room
4 Mechanical

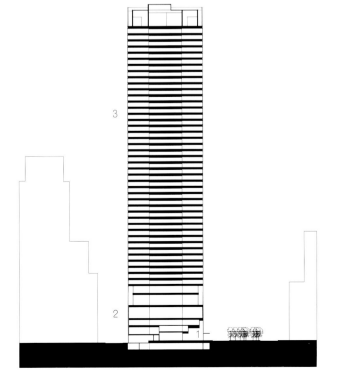

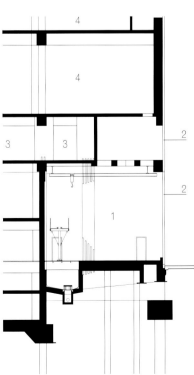

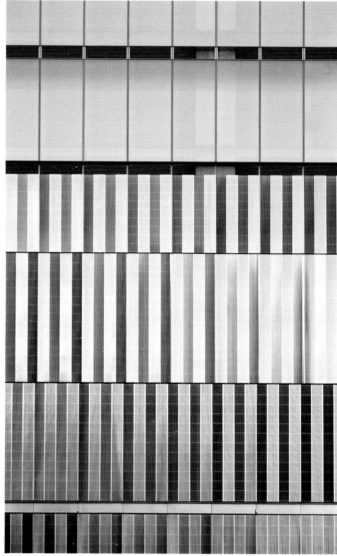

View through the tower.

View of the transition between the stainless-steel
podium screen and the glass curtain wall.

Wall plan detail and LED detail of the stainless-steel podium screen. The alignment of the triangular stainless-steel wires changes across the podium wall, creating bands with differing transparency and reflectivity.

1 Stainless-steel bar
2 Formed stainless-steel wire
3 Stainless-steel plate anchor bracket with vertically slotted holes
4 Cast-in-place concrete wall
5 Stainless-steel anchor embed
6 Custom LED fixture

Enlarged spandrel detail.
Façade section. The curtain wall was developed to maximize daylighting and minimize solar gain.
Façade elevation.

1 Typical wall unit (13' 6")
2 Low-iron glass with high performance coating and ceramic frit in gradient dot pattern
3 Handrail
4 Formed stainless-steel spandrel panel
5 Blue stainless-steel reflector
6 Top of slab

Pages 144–145:
View from the corner of Vesey and Greenwich Streets.

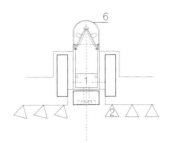

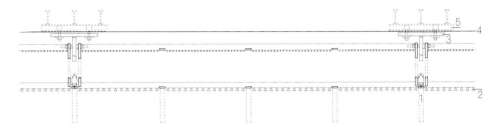

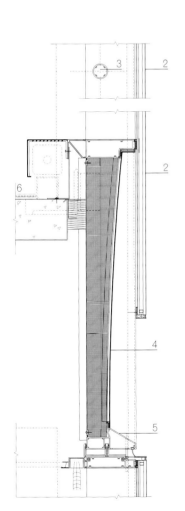

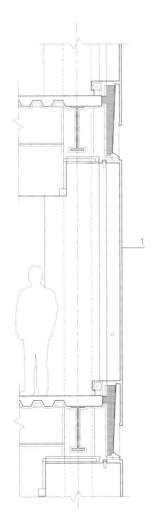

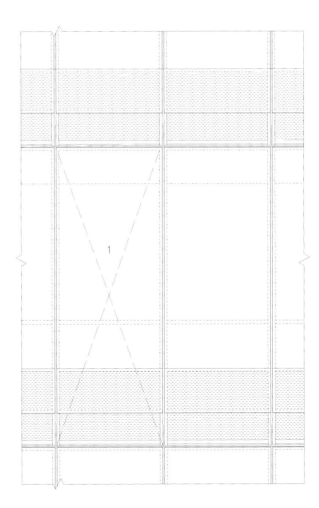

Al Rayyan Boulevard and Residential Development
Doha, Qatar, 2006

The master plan for Al Rayyan redefines the traditional boulevard by establishing a destination for retail, civic, and cultural functions. Located across from a park, the scheme brings together the main centers of commerce, government, and faith within the fabric of Qatar's most historically significant neighborhood.

The design is based on a series of harmonic curves inspired by the wave forms of the boulevard's diverse sounds, from the call to prayer at neighborhood mosques and local street music to the activity at a nearby souk. These arcs establish vehicular and pedestrian movements through the site and connect to the surrounding community.

The residential development is planned to provide community-oriented public space, including cafés, restaurants, and retail, and uninterrupted views of the corniche. An important feature of the plan is improved physical and visual access to both the park and wider surroundings. The entire historic district will be revitalized with strengthened infrastructure, new facilities, and a strong emphasis on pedestrian circulation.

Perspective view. The development provides uninterrupted views of the corniche and connections to the park.

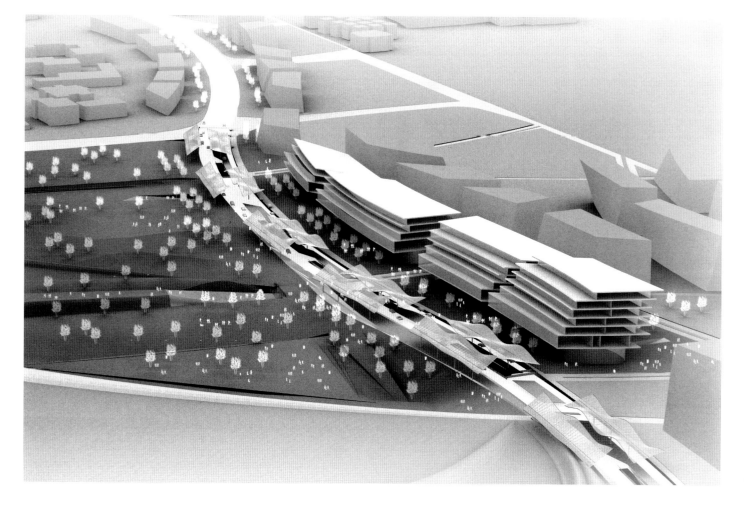

Al Rayyan Master Plan

Overall view of site. Al Rayyan Boulevard is
defined by a series of harmonic curves that
establishes vehicular and pedestrian movements, connecting these paths with the
surrounding community.

Alexandria Waterfront Redevelopment Project
Alexandria, Egypt, 2006

This master plan is intended to revitalize Alexandria's crescent-shaped Eastern Harbor by integrating historic sites, improving transport and pedestrian access, and creating new cultural, retail, and hospitality facilities. The East District enhances the area surrounding the Bibliotheca Alexandrina with a hotel and convention center, 20,000 square meters of retail, 17,500 square meters of offices, and a luxury hotel. Three museums, which make up an area radiating out toward the sea, allow convenient access to the ruins in the harbor and new pedestrian promenade along the corniche. The West District expands an area that currently has retail and market uses with an aquarium, hotel, 48,000 square meters of housing, and an additional 117,000 square meters of retail.

Linking the East and West development districts is the Arc of the Sun, which completes the circle implied by the curve of the waterfront. The arc provides new waterfront neighborhoods and, by forming a new breakwater, facilitates access to underwater ruins. Points of interest in the master plan are viewed as constellations. One of the most prominent is a solar power generator that takes the form of a delicate tower; at night, the glowing form recalls the ancient lighthouse of Alexandria, one of the seven wonders of the ancient world.

Aerial perspective. New connections link to a constellation of underwater ruins.

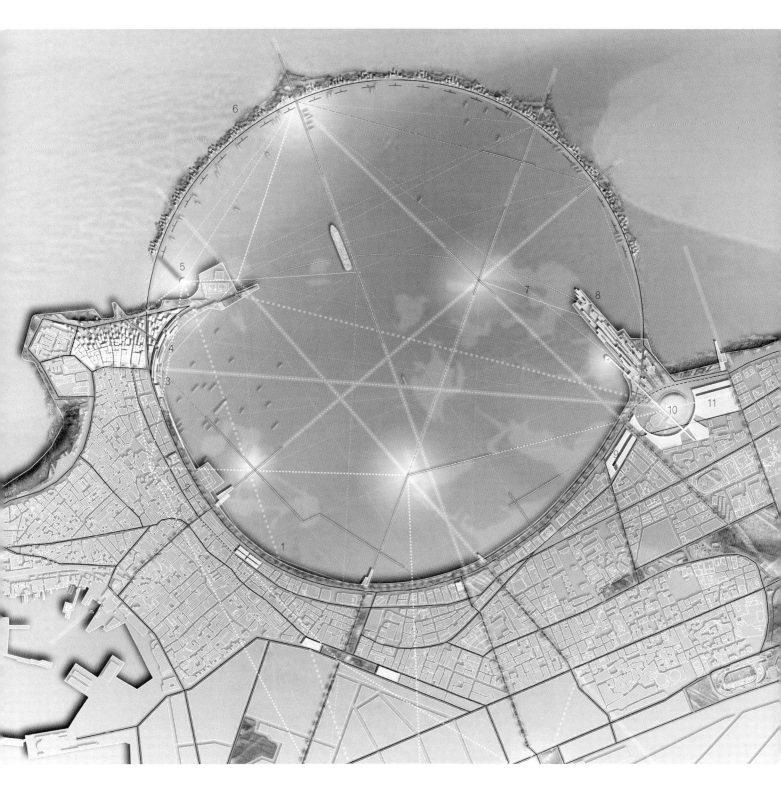

Plan. A crescent of new land acts as a breakwater
and completes the form of the harbor.

1 Boardwalk
2 Corniche
3 Retail marketplace
4 Aquarium
5 Solar tower
6 Resort, residential, hotel
7 Underwater ruins
8 Museum
9 Luxury hotel
10 Bibliotheca Alexandrina
11 Convention center and hotel

Boardwalk/corniche plan and sections. Variations in the profile of the harbor's perimeter create a dynamic experience for visitors. The rhythm of paving materials and planting changes to distinguish different neighborhoods around the corniche.

1 Corniche
2 Boardwalk
3 Floating pier

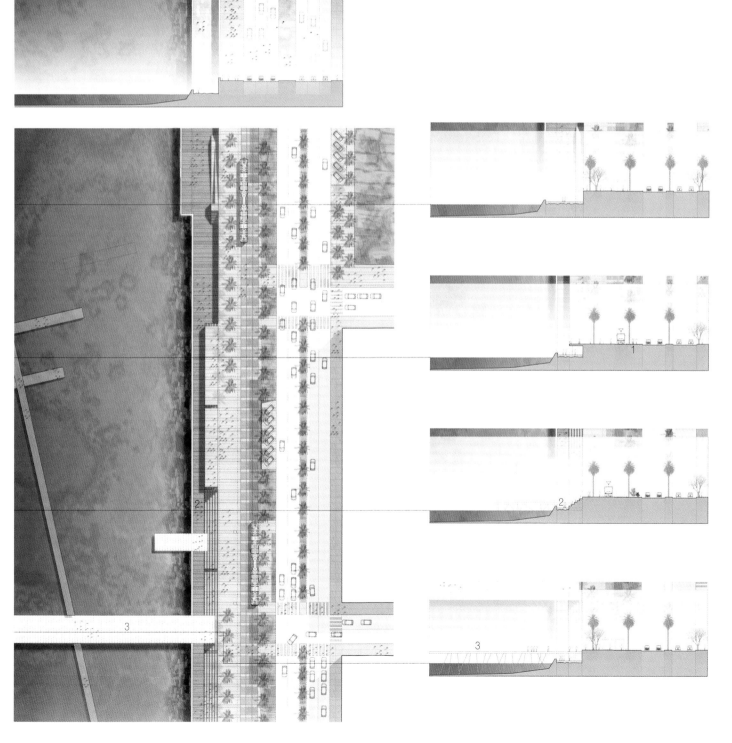

Proposed plan.
Existing plan.
1 Bibliotheca Alexandrina
2 Corniche
3 West district
4 Underwater ruins

Condé Nast Cafeteria
New York, New York, 2006

This cafeteria for the magazine publisher Condé Nast uses surfaces of dynamic light to create an immersive environment. Diners arrive via a luminous glass-walled corridor; embedded LEDs with motion sensors transform their movements into wall patterns. Inside the cafeteria, thousands of individually controlled LED nodes behind colorless glass cover the walls and ceilings. The twelve-thousand-square-foot space can change color throughout the day, mimicking natural sunlight or using a more dramatic palette of colors.

For those in need of a more private meal or work session, five blue niches with soft surfaces offer individual sound control. At the north side of the main dining room, acoustic fabric panels may be moved to reconfigure the space. Also providing a contrast in the otherwise glowing setting is the servery, in shades of dark and medium gray, including stainless-steel counters.

Plan.
1 Entry
2 LED corridor
3 Main dining room
4 Private dining room
5 Dish washing
6 Servery
7 Kitchen

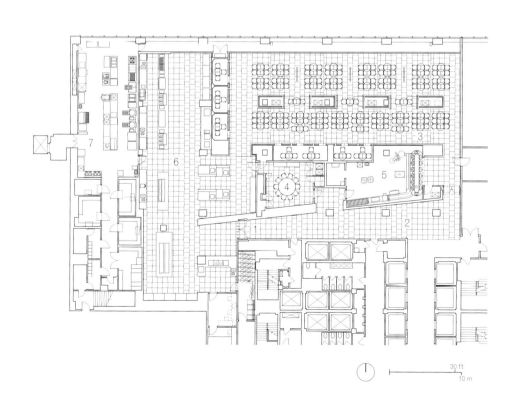

30 ft
10 m

The main dining room. The walls and ceiling are made of low-iron glass with diffusing interlayers; LED nodes are behind the colorless glass. The floors are ceramic tile.

Views of the main dining room. The lighting scheme, which includes thousands of LEDs that can be individually programmed, produces a range of color environments within the cafeteria and can be used to unify or divide the space.

Poly International Plaza
Guangzhou, China, 2006

Poly International Plaza overlooks the Pearl River in Pazhou, an industrial district in the city of Guangzhou. The 180,000-square-foot office and retail complex is comprised of two thirty-three-story office towers and two three-story mixed-use pavilions housing retail and exhibition facilities. The four structures are set in a landscaped court of plazas, water features, and park areas. Underneath the plaza are an exhibition hall and trade center. Teak-screened arcades on each side of the landscaped area link the towers and pavilions and serve as gateways to the complex.

The offices have fifteen-meter-wide floorplates, which are slender enough to admit daylight to the full depth of the workspace. The north facades, which are oriented to the river, are faced in glass with vertical fins. Reinforced-concrete X-bracing, part of the structural spine on the south facades, shades the offices and maximizes the amount of column-free space inside. Offset vertical elevator and service cores are encased in translucent and opalescent glass, making visible the activity within and allowing views from the elevator cabs and lobbies of the surrounding district. A three-story horizontal opening perforates each tower at its midpoint, forming large central employee terraces that also reduce the buildings' wind load.

View from the south. ▷

Site plan.
 1 North tower lobby
 2 Open air terrace
 3 Auto drop-off
 4 Visitor parking
 5 Water feature
 6 Central garden
 7 Access to exhibition center
 8 Skylight water feature
 9 Palm grove
10 Meeting, conference, retail
11 Exhibition and low-rise office entry
12 South tower lobby
13 Covered arcade
14 Service and parking access ramp

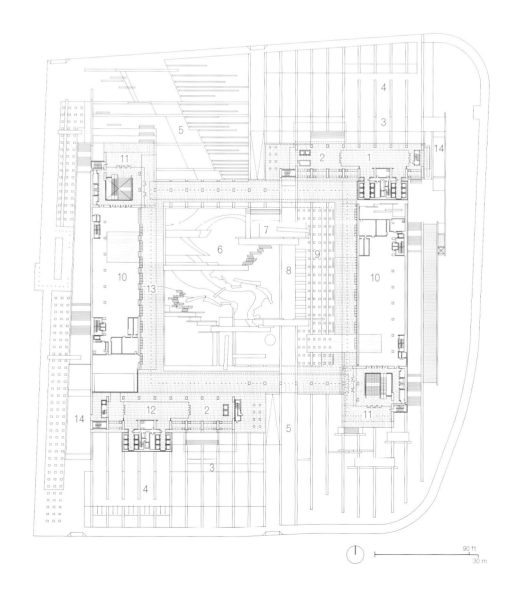

90 ft
30 m

保利国际广场 | POLY INTERNATIONAL PLAZA

◁ View of the south facade of the south building. The exposed structural lattice also provides sunshading.

View from the north. The north facades, floor-to-ceiling glass, are shaded by vertical fins. Each building has a large aperture at its midpoint, which allows wind to pass through, lessening stresses on the structure, and serves as an emergency area of refuge.

Plan, typical office tower floor.
 1 Office
 2 Glass-enclosed elevator lobby
 3 Structural lattice
 4 Mechanical
 5 Electrical
 6 Telecom
 7 Restroom
 8 Janitorial
 9 Service elevator
10 Balcony

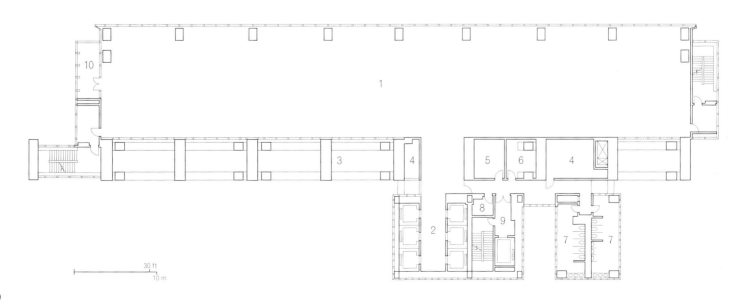

30 ft
10 m

View of the central garden and exhibition and retail spaces.

View of an entry lobby. ▷

Section through office tower and podium building.
1 Office
2 Refuge terrace with lounge and meeting facility above
3 Lobby
4 Glazed core
5 Exhibition and retail
6 Below-grade exhibition and parking

Night view from the southwest. The lighting ▷ enhances the volumetric nature of the large-scale structural lattice.

View of an elevator lobby. The elevators are set within the glass-clad vertical cores of each tower.

Section through typical floor.
1 Corridor
2 Air highway
3 Raised access floor
4 Cabling
5 Floor diffuser
6 Air supply
7 Perimeter zone
8 Perimeter diffuser
9 Variable air volume unit
10 Indirect/direct diffuser
11 Exposed beams
12 Metal acoustical ceiling
13 Air return

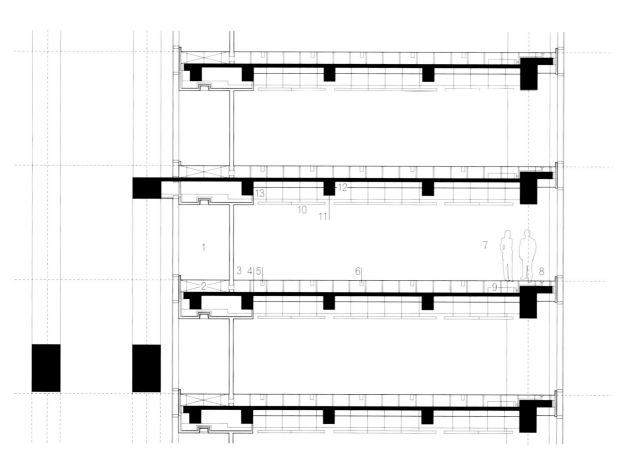

Treasure Island
San Francisco, California, 2006

Located in the center of San Francisco Bay, Treasure Island was once the site of the 1939 Golden Gate International Exposition. Until recently, the artificial island served as a part of a naval base, along with areas of Yerba Buena Island, to which it is connected by an isthmus. The new master plan redevelops Treasure Island and a portion of Yerba Buena Island as a dense, transit-oriented residential community with areas of cultural and commercial interest and ferry connections to San Francisco.

Among the features of the new community are compact neighborhoods, which encourage walking and cycling; an organic farm and reconstructed wetlands; and an extensive program of green buildings. Design strategies focus on sustainability, minimizing energy consumption, planting open spaces with native vegetation, and providing infrastructure for the generation of renewable energy. Treasure Island's unique microclimate—the low-lying island is relatively flat and experiences strong winds—is mitigated by a strategy of shifting the street grid and siting buildings and green spaces to shelter pedestrians and public spaces.

Commercial, retail, and cultural components developed as part of the master plan attract both visitors and residents. A combination of historic buildings adapted to current uses and new buildings gives the island a visual identity. On the west side is an urban core, with the ferry terminal, retail plaza, and group of towers; the tallest, Sun Tower, is inspired by the iconic tower built for the 1939 exposition. The slender towers let daylight pass to open spaces and together form a delicate skyline visible from San Francisco and the East Bay.

Master plan.
 1 Ferry terminal
 2 Cityside residential area
 3 Urban core
 4 East side residential area
 5 Shoreline art park
 6 Shoreline park
 7 Ecological park
 8 Regional sports park
 9 Urban farm
10 Water recreation and access
11 Wastewater treatment plant
12 Job Corps (not part of Treasure Island project)
13 Historic buildings to remain

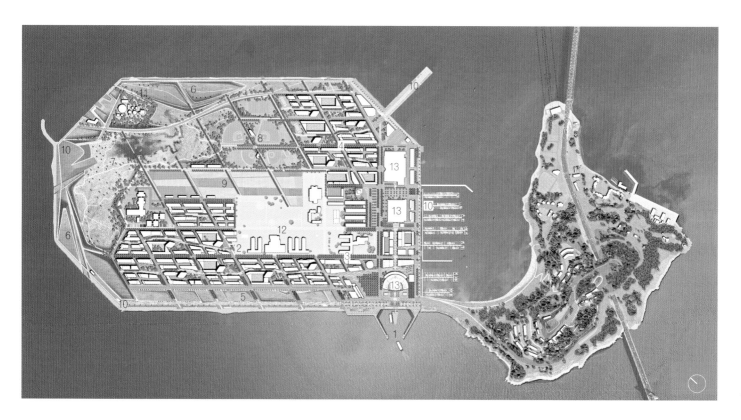

Perspective view of Treasure Island. The planning of the island as a whole is sensitive to the massing and placement of buildings in each neighborhood.

Aerial view of San Francisco, the Bay Bridge, Yerba Buena Island, and Treasure Island.

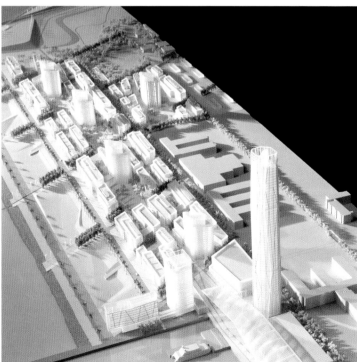

Aerial view of Cityside residential area with Sun Tower and ferry terminal in the foreground. Interlocking landscape zones and pedestrian walkways define neighborhood blocks.

Diagram of solar-oriented public space. An angled street grid superimposed on a conventional orthogonal grid diffuses the prevailing winds and takes advantage of the southern sun. Open spaces are strategically located where prevailing winds are blocked.

Diagram of wind-protected public space. Wind rows composed of trees and buildings deflect the wind in open spaces and neighborhoods.

Diagram of visitors' and residents' pathways. A hierarchy of streets reduces vehicular traffic in the residential neighborhoods.

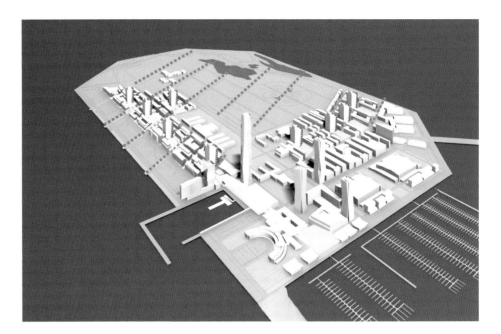

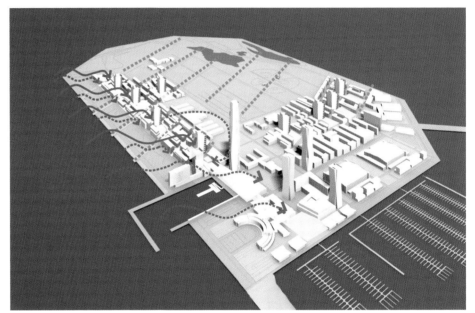

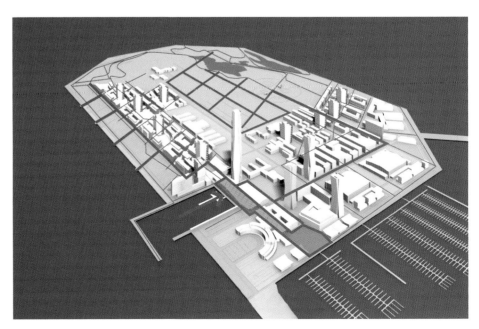

New Beijing Poly Plaza
Beijing, China, 2007

New Beijing Poly Plaza is located on Beijing's Second Ring Road, northeast of the Forbidden City. Built for the state-owned conglomerate China Poly, the hundred-thousand-square-meter building faces both a prominent intersection and the enterprise's existing headquarters. It serves as an executive headquarters, provides speculative office space, and, most prominently, features a museum of Chinese antiquities.

The building has a monumental triangular form, with an L-shaped office plan wrapping around a ninety-meter-high atrium. At the northeast facade, a cable-net curtain wall admits an abundance of daylight and presents a transparency and openness to the city. A glass lantern-like structure hangs inside the atrium and also passes through the curtain wall; housing the wood-clad Poly Art Museum, it is suspended by four steel cables, which reduce the effective span of the cable-net system and define the facets in the glass wall. The south and west facades have a travertine fin-wall brise-soleil that shades the glazed office space. A fifty-meter-high wall of bronze panels at the south entry facade allude to the ancient bronze artworks in the museum's collection. These panels, along with exterior stone fins, the cable-net wall, and pleated, patterned glass lantern, offer contrasting textures that respond to the Beijing climate, express the programs within, and suggest a symbolic relationship of the company to the city.

View of the south facade. ▷

Site plan.
1 North plaza and subway access
2 North entry
3 Atrium
4 South entry
5 Lounge and café
6 Office elevator lobby
7 Museum lobby
8 Bank
9 Parking ramp

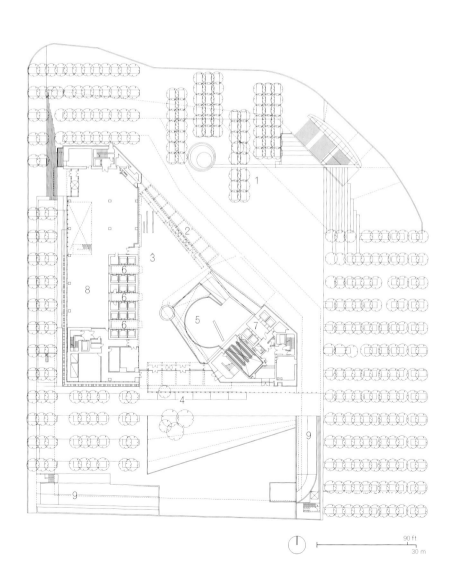

90 ft
30 m

View from the north. The main cable-net wall faces the Second Ring Road. The glass lantern, which houses the Poly Art Museum, intersects the curtain wall.

◁ View of the south facade. At night, the stone brise-soleil is illuminated, and the steel-and-glass lantern glows within.

Section.
1 Typical office floor
2 Upper part of atrium
3 Cable-net wall with hangers
4 Lounge
5 Museum, galleries, restaurant
6 Lower portion of atrium
7 South entry and drop-off
8 Lounge and cafeteria
9 North plaza
10 Retail and subway access
11 Parking and mechanical
12 Rooftop court
13 Boardroom

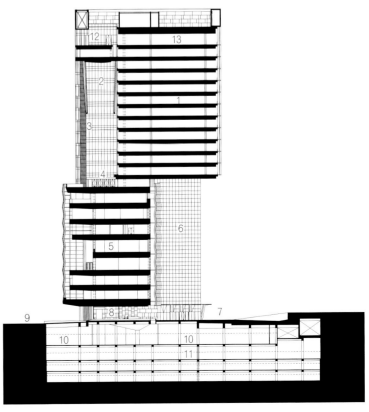

Views of the lobby with the museum lantern.

Lobby. The walls are travertine. ▷

Plan, typical low-rise floor.
Plan, typical high-rise floor.
 1 Exhibition space
 2 Gift shop
 3 Lobby
 4 Fire shutters
 5 Electrical
 6 Offices
 7 Telecom
 8 Air-handling facilities
 9 Northeast (primary) cable-net facade
10 South (secondary) cable-net facade
11 Open to area below
12 Main hanger cables
13 Rocker mechanism

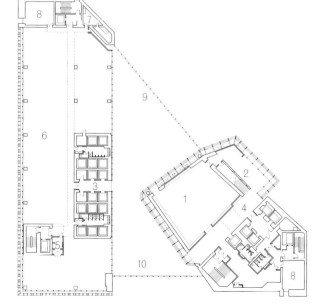

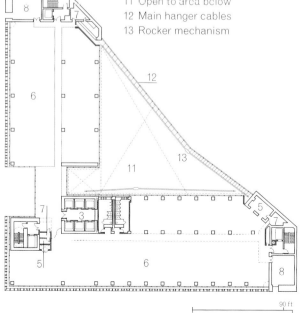

90 ft
30 m

Views of the south and west facades. Each facade has a travertine brise-soleil that shades floor-to-ceiling window walls.

Details of the brise-soleil.
Typical floor section.
1 Travertine brise-soleil
2 Window wall
3 Operable window
4 Cantilevered outrigger and grating with integrated linear lighting
5 Interior office space

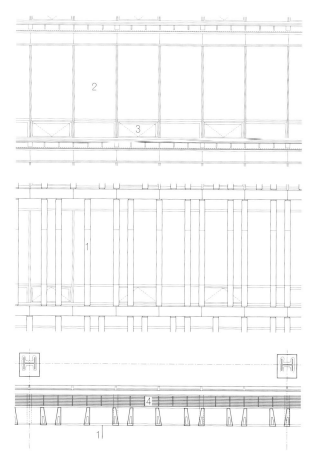

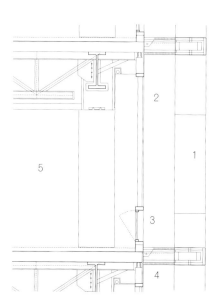

Detail of rocker mechanism, which allows for movement of the cables.

View of public gathering space atop the lantern.

View of the V-cable and cast-steel rocker mechanism, which stabilize the cable-net wall.

Section of rocker system.

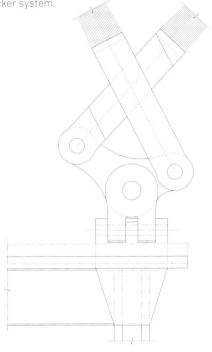

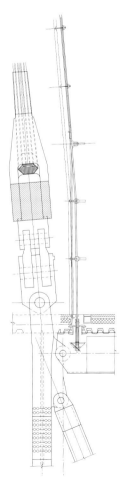

Changi International Airport: Terminal 3
Changi, Singapore, 2007

Terminal 3 was built as the third and final phase of Changi International Airport's master plan. In keeping with the Singaporean government's desire for an efficient terminal, the building is simple in plan. Its roof, however, is complex—a large, shimmering structure that modulates natural light. The 22-acre steel-truss-supported flat roof has 1,100 glass skylights and 215,000 interior and exterior perforated-aluminum louvers. The skylights and louvers allow the facility to be naturally illuminated during daytime hours.
While the thousands of louvers appear to be randomly placed, their locations were determined by a computer-generated pattern of repeating segments. The exterior louvers are motor-driven; activated by sensors, they control the amount of direct sunlight hitting the terminal floor. The interior louvers, fixed at set angles, are supported by a system of cables that also braces the roof structure. They reflect and diffuse light, help control acoustics, and give the interior a soft, organic feel.

Site plan.
1 Terminal 1
2 Terminal 2
3 Terminal 3
4 Rail Terminal
5 Airport Boulevard

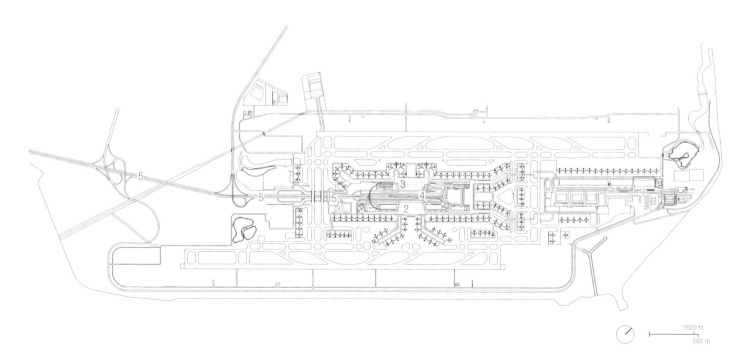

1500 ft
500 m

View of the ticketing hall. Natural light enters
the space through a network of skylights and
perforated-aluminum louvers above and below
the roof.

View toward the terminal from Airport Boulevard.

View of the main roof over the ticketing area ▷
and departure hall. The perforated-aluminum
louvers animate the ceiling.

Section.
1 Departures level
2 Arrivals level
3 Departures concourse
4 Retail
5 Baggage claim
6 Ticketing

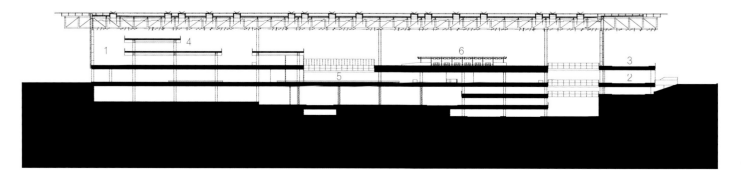

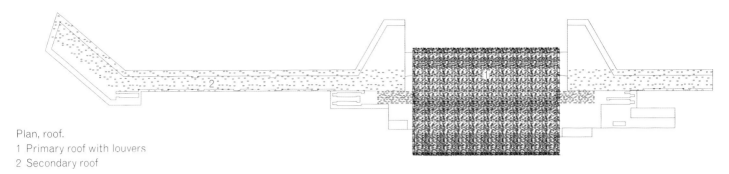

Plan, roof.
1 Primary roof with louvers
2 Secondary roof

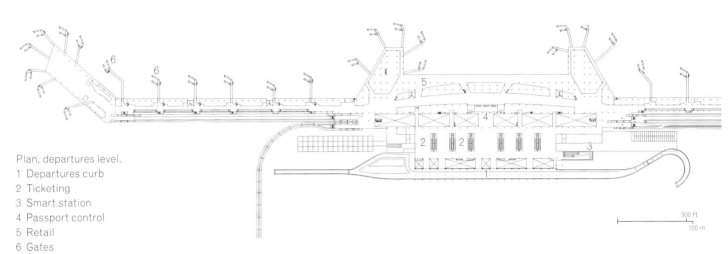

Plan, departures level.
1 Departures curb
2 Ticketing
3 Smart station
4 Passport control
5 Retail
6 Gates

300 ft
100 m

◁ View of the baggage claim area. The claim itself as well as the wall has been landscaped.

View of the terminal roof showing the operable louvers that automatically adjust to maintain a consistent amount of daylight in the building.

Exploded axonometric of the louvered roof assembly.
Detail section through skylight and louver assembly.
1 Operable aluminum louvers
2 Grating panel
3 Aluminum secondary roof framing
4 Prefabricated skylight unit
5 Membrane roof
6 Suspended metal ceiling
7 Skylight reflector panel
8 Truss
9 Horizontal reflector panel
10 Tensioned louver suspension cable
11 Aluminum louver support
12 Perforated-aluminum louver
13 Steel girder
14 Metal deck
15 Roof ridge beyond

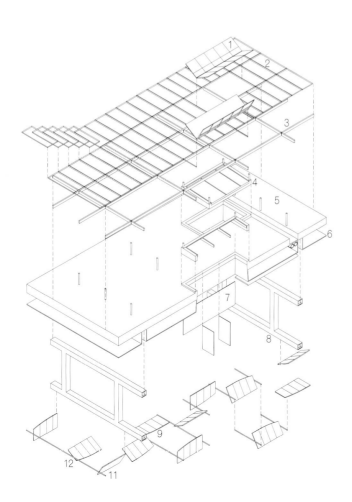

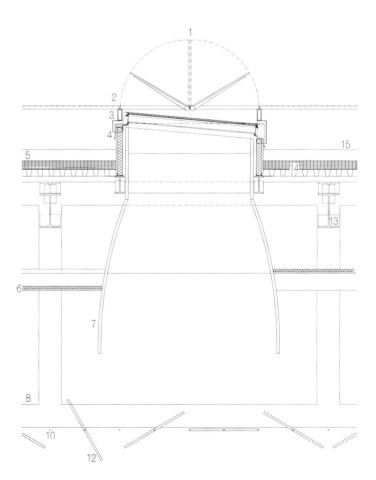

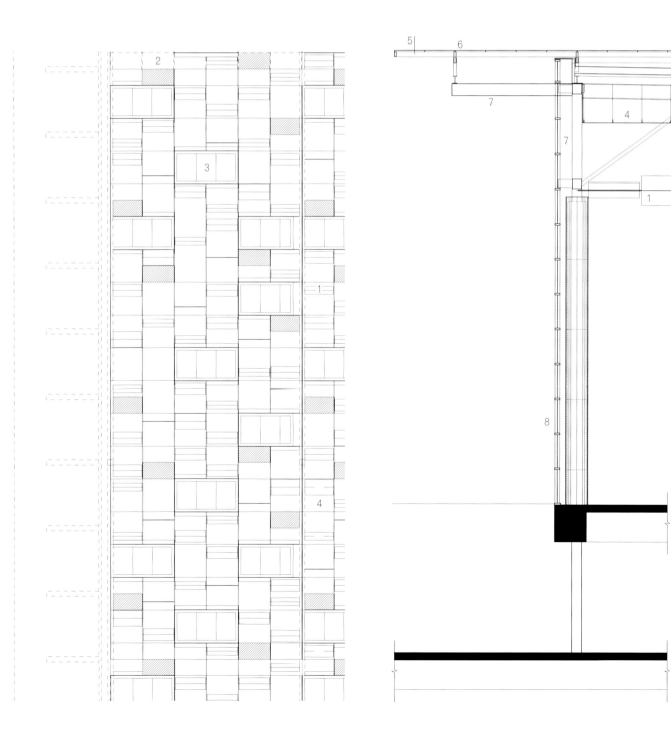

Reflected ceiling plan, detail of main roof.
Although the pattern of the ceiling panels and
louvers repeats, the impression is one of a
random arrangement.
Detail section at exterior wall.
1 Perforated-aluminum louver
2 Horizontal reflective louver
3 Skylight
4 Suspended metal ceiling panel
5 Grating panel
6 Aluminum secondary floor framing
7 Steel structural framing
8 Exterior wall

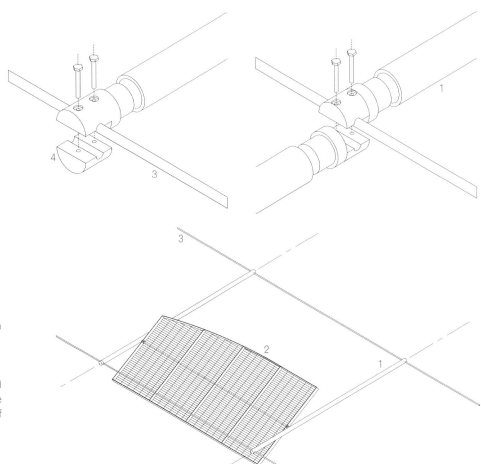

View of the lightweight perforated-aluminum composite louvers.

Panel support connection detail.
Panel support detail. A system of cables suspended between the structural trusses supports the interior louvers while also stabilizing the roof trusses.
1 Aluminum tube
2 Perforated-aluminum louver
3 Suspension cable

4 Cast-aluminum fitting

Deerfield Academy: Koch Center for Science, Math & Technology
Deerfield, Massachusetts, 2007

The eighty-thousand-square-foot science center for Deerfield Academy encourages informal and formal learning as well as cross-disciplinary relationships. Housed in the LEED-Gold-certified building are classroom and laboratory facilities for math and the sciences along with two biology and growth garden rooms, café, lecture hall, and a fifty-seat planetarium.

The siting of the building integrates the grade change between the higher and lower levels of the campus, and its curved exterior walls serve as retaining walls. This close relationship between architecture and landscape is reiterated by the turf roof. The building is clad in red brick in keeping with Deerfield's master plan. Classroom windows are arranged across the curved facades, responding to the interior layout, which is organized along three hallways.

At the building's center is the science commons, which acts as circulation space, gathering space, café, and public lobby for the building. Inset into the roof is an angled analemma skylight that projects a ray of light onto the thirty-foot wall of the commons. Tracked by student markings over a year, that projection of the sun's rays creates a figure eight. A star field map—northern hemisphere on the ceiling, southern hemisphere on the floor—illuminated with lighting designed by artist James Turrell, shows what the skies will look like in the year 2040, when the northern hemisphere planets converge into one focused area.

Site plan.
1 Koch Center for Science, Math & Technology
2 Boyden Library
3 Athletic field
4 Baseball field
5 Parking

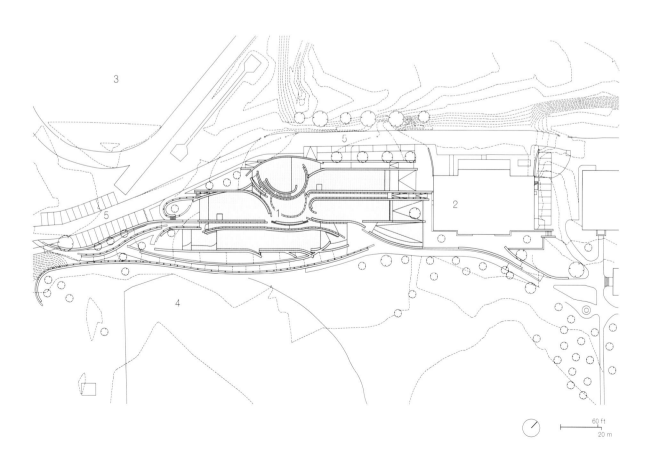

60 ft
20 m

The main entrance.

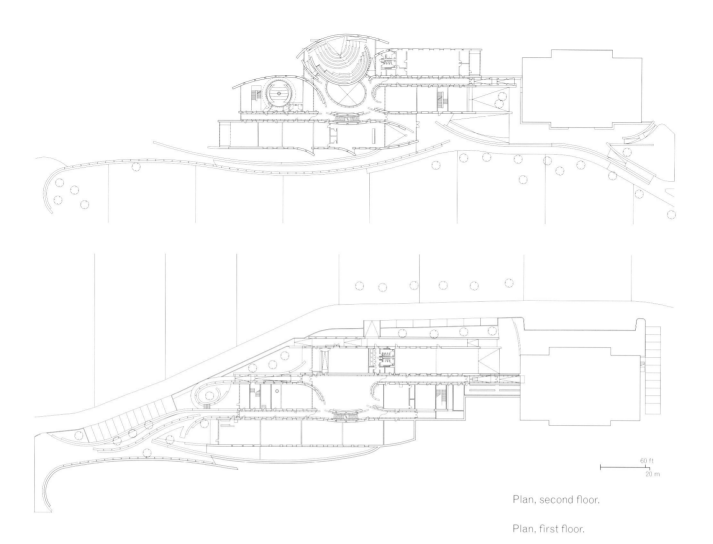

Plan, second floor.

Plan, first floor.

View from the northwest.

Aerial view from the southeast.

Section.
1 Math department
2 Science department
3 Biochemistry laboratory
4 Stair
5 Analemma skylight
6 Analemma wall
7 Science commons
8 Atrium
9 Star terrace
10 Auditorium
11 Mechanical

Detail section through the analemma skylight.
1 Lowest sun angle: December 21
2 Highest sun angle: June 21
3 Projection onto wall
4 Elevation of analemma aperture

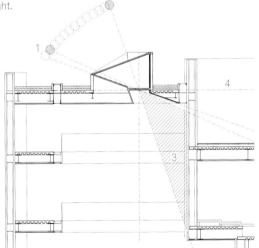

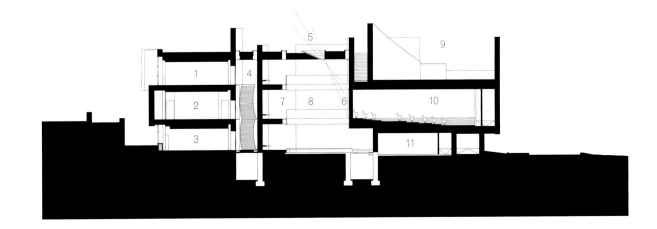

◁ The ceiling of the science commons. The fiber-optic lights portray the celestial view from the Northern Hemisphere on September 9, 2040, a time when the planets will converge into one small area.

View of the science commons, which serves as a circulation space and also as a public lobby.

View of glazing set into curved, red-brick walls.

Harvard University: Northwest Science Building
Cambridge, Massachusetts, 2008

Harvard University had just one plot of underutilized land remaining on its historic campus to dedicate to this new science building, which provides an inventive model for educational facilities by bringing together experts from diverse fields, including neuroscience, bioengineering, systems biology, and computational biology. One of the university's goals was to maximize utilization of the site, which weaves between six existing buildings and faces a residential neighborhood.

SOM created a flexible building appropriate in scale to its neighbors and sympathetic to the organizational structure and architectural language of the campus. A substantial portion of the building—more than half of the square footage—sits below-grade. The 530,000-square-foot building incorporates three functioning green roofs and harmonizes with its residential and human-scale surroundings.

The structure, with its network of passages and gathering spaces, fosters a strongly connected community and emphasizes cross-disciplinary research by engendering a free exchange of ideas. The collegial spaces, informal double-height "living rooms" along easy paths of travel, infuse the building with energy. The final building addresses the challenges of program and site in a collaborative environment that is designed to attract high-caliber researchers, faculty, and students to Harvard.

Exterior view of the circulation hub. The hub ▷ represents the physical connection across the sciences.

Site plan.
1 Northwest Science Building
2 Harvard Museum of Natural History
3 Museum of Comparative Zoology lab
4 New museum yard
5 Future development
6 Buffer park
7 Hammond Street

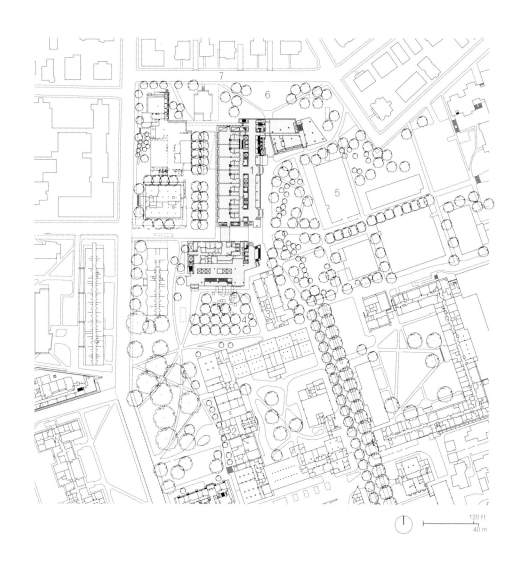

120 ft
40 m

Section.
1 Pedagogical area
2 Lab office
3 Wet labs
4 Harvard collections
5 Lab space
6 Intake shaft
7 Exhaust shaft
8 Central plant cooling towers
9 Mechanical
10 Existing parking garage

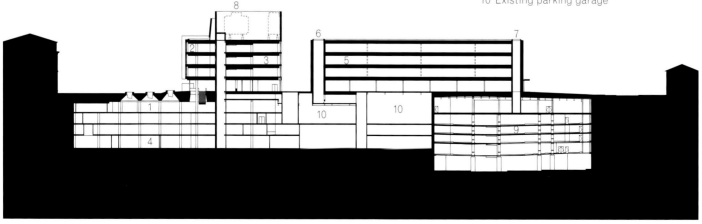

◁ View from the northeast. Two-story lounges create spatial complexity and set aside social places for researchers to meet and interact.

Night view from the south. The new Science Building serves to define a new South Yard. The south entry is situated along an axis that links the building to the science facilities across Oxford Street.

The new museum yard and south facade. The landscape furniture in the yard, positioned around skylights for the below-ground levels of the science building, fosters casual outdoor meetings.

Interior view of "living room" lounge. These large, open gathering spaces encourage the cross-pollination of ideas.

View of the new museum yard. A considerable portion of the building sits below grade to preserve the pedestrian scale of the campus and create new, active green spaces.

Interior view of the main entry. Multiple building ▷ entries encourage movement through, instead of around, the structure and preserve the open and interconnected nature of the campus.

View of the vertical circulation hub. The stair ▷ draws daylight into the building and provides campus views to the students and researchers.

Plan, ground floor.
1 Teaching labs
2 Facilities offices and receiving
3 Café
4 Main entry
5 New museum yard
6 Buffer park

Plan, second floor.
1 Wet labs
2 Dry labs/Offices
3 Lounge
4 Main vertical circulation hub
5 Museum of Comparative Zoology lab

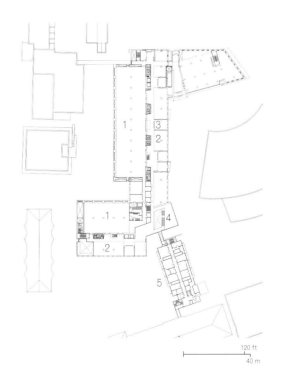

120 ft
40 m

Lester B. Pearson International Airport: New Terminal 1
Toronto, Canada, 2007

The new Terminal 1 is part of an expansion that will allow Toronto's Lester B. Pearson International Airport to serve an estimated 39 million passengers annually by the year 2015. It replaces two existing terminals with a single facility that features a grand daylit space and, through the use of texture and light, intuitive wayfinding for travelers. Together with four pier buildings that extend out to the airfield, it has an area of four million square feet and provides seventy-seven boarding gates. A high-speed baggage-handling system moves luggage from check-in desks to waiting aircraft.

Throughout the terminal, expressed structural elements are contrasted with light glass elements to delineate zones and provide a welcoming environment. In the curved departures hall, linear skylights align with the aisles between ticketing islands, and concrete buttresses support white-painted steel armatures that hold up the long-span roof. Glass floors mark the transition to the departure gates. The arrivals hall has a similar language, with heavy buttresses set under two-story light wells formed by offset roof panels. A balcony overlooks the baggage claim hall, offering a sense of orientation upon arrival. An extensive art program, including large-scale installations by Sol LeWitt and Richard Serra, provides visual breaks within the large facility.

Site plan.
1 Terminal 1
2 Pier A (existing)
3 Pier B (existing)
4 Pier C (existing)
5 Pier D
6 Pier E
7 Pier F
8 Pier G (future expansion)
9 Pedestrian bridges
10 Automated people-mover station
11 Parking garage

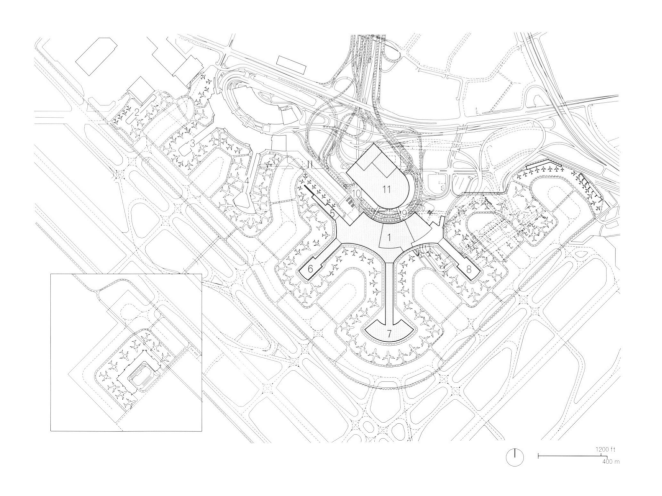

View of the curved terminal from the three-level roadway. An enclosed bridge leads from the terminal to the parking garage on the right.

Night view of the departures hall from the west.

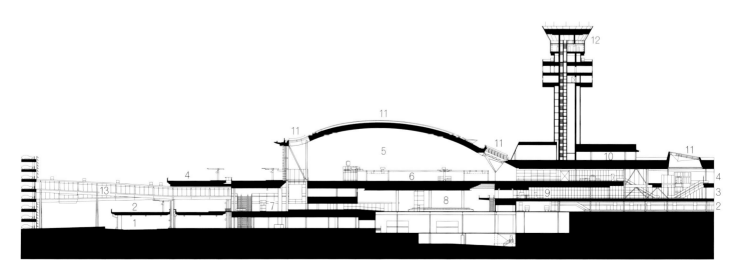

◁ Section.

View of the concrete buttresses in the departures hall. The white-painted-steel structural "wishbones" support glazed roof panels that form two-story light wells.

Plan, third level. ▷
1 Domestic check-in
2 International check-in
3 U.S.-bound (transborder) check-in
4 U.S. customs border patrol
5 U.S. baggage drop-off
6 Security
7 Pier D
8 Pier E
9 Pier F
10 Pier G (future expansion)

Plan, first level. ▷
1 Domestic baggage claim
2 International baggage claim
3 Canadian customs
4 Secondary customs
5 Domestic arrivals hall
6 International arrivals hall
7 Arrival baggage roadway
8 Airside bus lobby
9 Departure baggage make-up
10 Seating/gate area
11 Service/mechanical

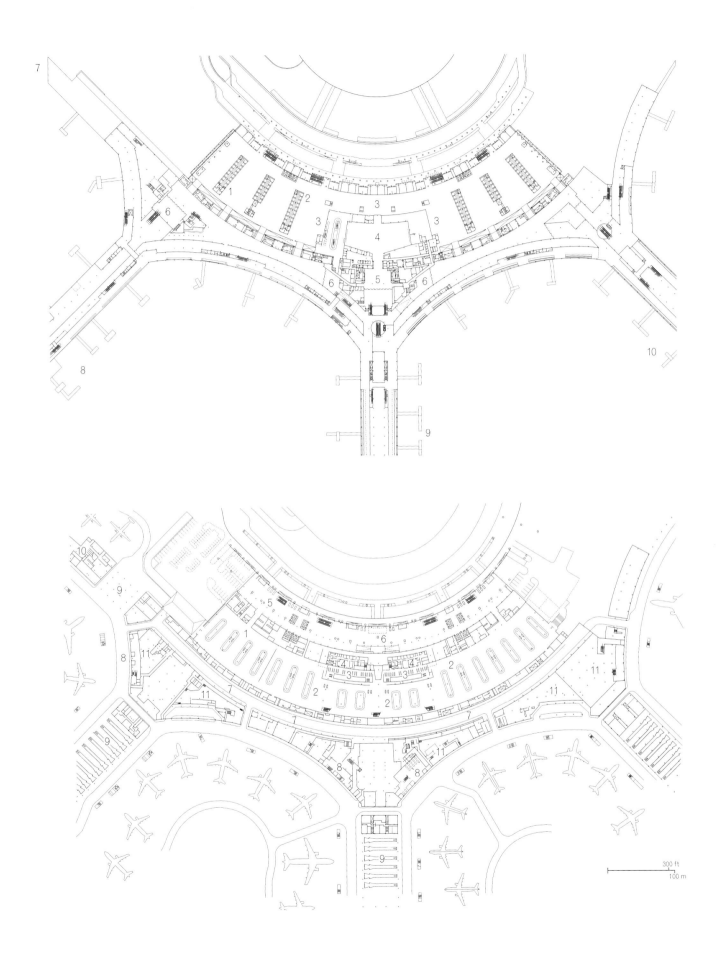

Views of artworks in the terminal. The installations allude to flight and movement.
1 Jonathan Borofsky, *I Dreamed I Could Fly*, 2003
2 Richard Serra, *Tilted Spheres*, 2002–4
3 Sol LeWitt, *Wall Drawing #1100, Concentric Bands*, 2003

Detail section at skylight above steel structural "wishbone."

1 Skylight
2 Ventilation louver
3 Steel girder
4 Gutter
5 Maintenance track system
6 Sun protection louvers
7 Steel wishbone structure
8 Concrete buttress

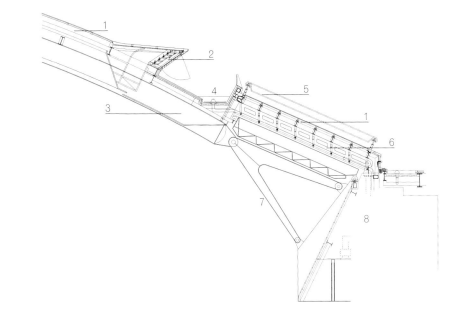

View into departures hall from a glass-floored bridge. A steel "wishbone" stretches above, bracing the roof panels.

View of the departures hall on the third level. Linear skylights in the curved roof modulate the vast space and help orient passengers.

Tokyo Midtown
Tokyo, Japan, 2007

Located in the heart of Tokyo, a city known for its vibrant street life and dense architecture, Tokyo Midtown is a cluster of six buildings set on former Defense Agency land.
The plot, once walled off from the city, had been empty for sixty years; the new twenty-
five-acre complex reintegrates the area into the urban context while providing the busy
metropolis with public green space.

The master plan allocates five million square feet to mixed-use development, including
luxury apartments, hotel, office space, convention and conference space, shopping
center, and the Suntory Museum of Art, and places a five-acre park in the north portion
of the site. Three office towers, Midtown East, Midtown West, and Midtown Tower,
surround a main plaza with a steel-and-glass canopy. Midtown Tower has fifty-three
floors, with a Ritz-Carlton hotel on the top levels. At the time of its completion, it was
the tallest building in Tokyo. The two lower buildings act as foothills, in an allusion to
traditional Japanese garden design.

Inspired by Japanese shoji screens, the facades are layered, overlapping in various ways
to create a distinct visual identity for each of the three buildings. At the north and south
facades of Midtown Tower, vertical glass "sails" rise past the roofline, breaking up the
building's width, emphasizing its vertical rise, and aligning it with the ground-level plaza.
At the top levels, the glass planes, angled to resemble a woven surface, catch sunlight
to create a reflective beacon and extend the building's verticality.

View into the plaza from the southwest. ▷
Midtown Tower is in the center, with Midtown
West on the left and Midtown East on the right.

Site plan.
1 Midtown Tower
2 Midtown East
3 Midtown West
4 Plaza
5 Canopy

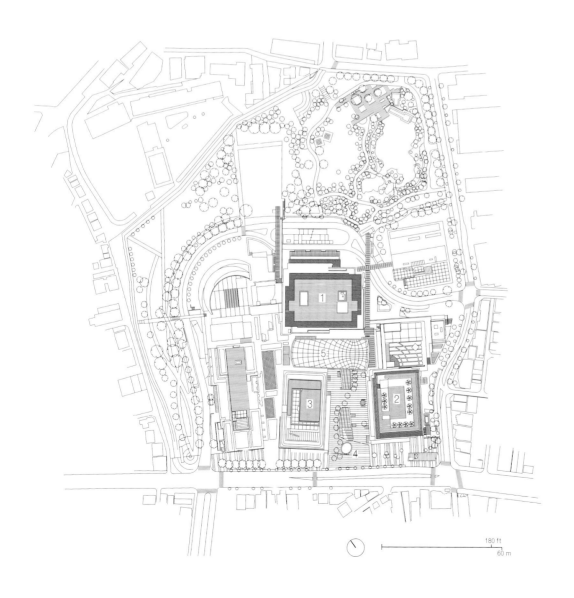

180 ft
60 m

204

Night view of the plaza.

View of the top of Midtown Tower. On the right is one of the building's two vertical glass "sails." The angled glass panels recall traditional Japanese weaving.

Plan, fifth floor.
Plan, ground floor.

 1 Park Residences at the Ritz-Carlton Tokyo
 2 Tokyo Midtown Residence entrance
 3 Oakwood Premium Tokyo Midtown Residences
 4 Oakwood Premium Tokyo Midtown Residence
   entrance
 5 Office
 6 Suntory Museum
 7 Rooftop garden
 8 Plaza
 9 Retail
10 Subway entrance
11 Ritz-Carlton Tokyo
12 Hotel vestibule
13 Office entrance lobby
14 Hotel café
15 Shuttle elevator lobby
16 Galleria
17 Suntory Museum entrance

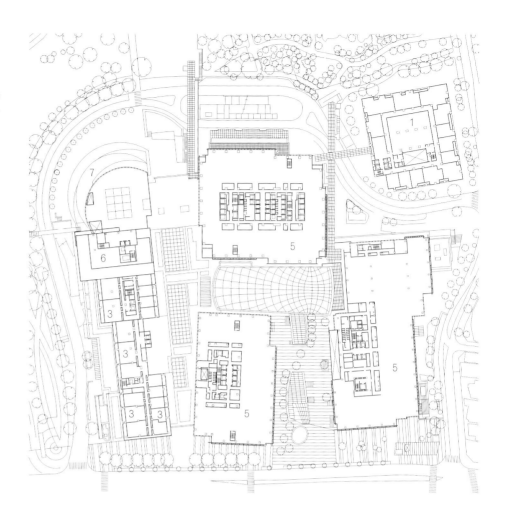

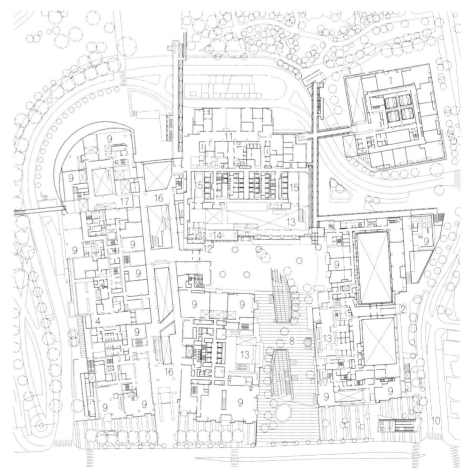

90 ft
30 m

Overall section.
1 Residences
2 Offices
3 Plaza
4 Entrance hall
5 Roof garden
6 Galleria
7 Auditorium
8 Concourse

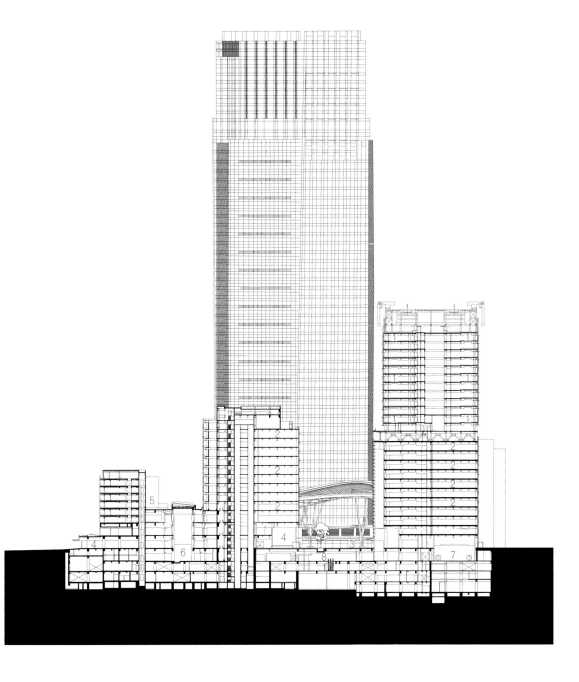

View from the galleria to the plaza.

Section through Midtown Tower and Midtown West.
 1 Office
 2 Hotel
 3 Entrance hall
 4 Entrance lobby
 5 Hotel skylobby
 6 Pool
 7 Event room
 8 Meeting zone
 9 Grand ballroom
10 Terrace
11 Promenade
12 Vestibule
13 Hotel drop-off

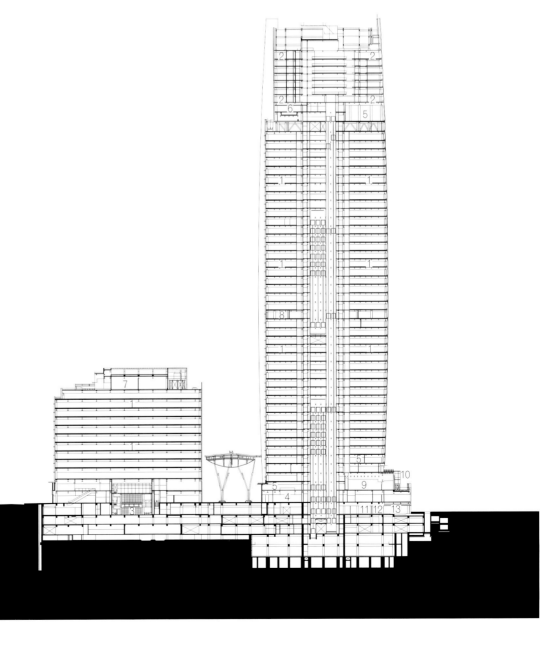

View of the concourse level of the plaza. Midtown Tower can be seen through the skylight. The stone sculpture, *Shape of Mind*, is by Kan Yasuda.

Takenobu Igarashi's sculpture *to the sea of premonition* hangs in Midtown Tower's entrance lobby.

The Midtown Tower entrance lobby.

Pages 212–213:
Aerial view from the southwest.

U.S. Census Bureau Headquarters
Suitland, Maryland, 2007

Situated on thirty wooded acres of the Suitland Federal Center near downtown Washington, D.C., the 1.5-million-square-foot headquarters for the U.S. Census Bureau provides a unified low-rise campus for the agency's six thousand regular employees as well as for the numerous additional staff who help with the census-taking every ten years. Designed to LEED Gold specifications, the complex employs many sustainable strategies, including water reclamation, use of recycled materials, minimal energy consumption, and natural daylighting.

A guiding principle of the design was mitigating the structure's size and impact on the landscape. The building is split into two eight-story bars, each 1,100 feet long. They are curved in plan so that they do not appear monolithic, and they are narrow enough to let daylight permeate each floorplate. The exterior facade is softened by a brise-soleil of white oak fins; behind this "veil" are green-tinted precast spandrels and glazed vision panels. Inside, central amenities like the library, gym, and medical facilities are organized along an internal street that runs through the complex. The open-plan offices are calibrated to accommodate the variable number of workers. Large volumes—the cafeteria, conference center, and auditorium—project out from internal street through the west facade. Facing the courtyard are two-story community areas with lounges and other support areas. Color is used throughout the interior to provide wayfinding and a sense of organization; the palette ranges from natural hues close to the curtain wall to more vibrant tones at the core.

Site plan.
1 U.S. Census Bureau
2 Suitland Metro Station
3 Metro parking
4 Silver Hill Road
5 Woodland preserve

360 ft
120 m

View from the west. The bar buildings are
curved to disguise their length.

◁ Detail view of the wood brise-soleil. The curved white oak blades are attached to the precast-concrete facade with stainless-steel frames.

View from the east. On the east facade, large black letters painted on the wood fins spell the agency's name.

View of intersecting brise-soleils.

Detail section of facade.
1 Tubular steel with intumescent paint
2 Mullion
3 Panel frame

Exterior elevation and section, showing the white oak blades.

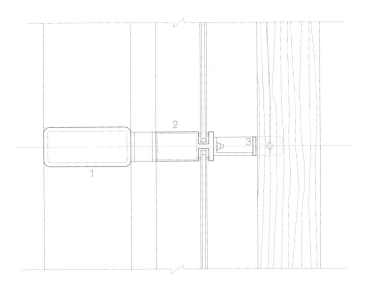

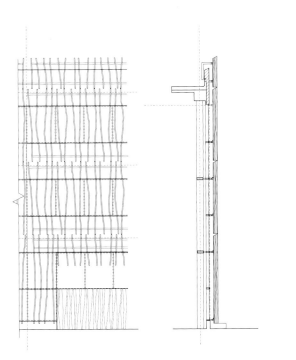

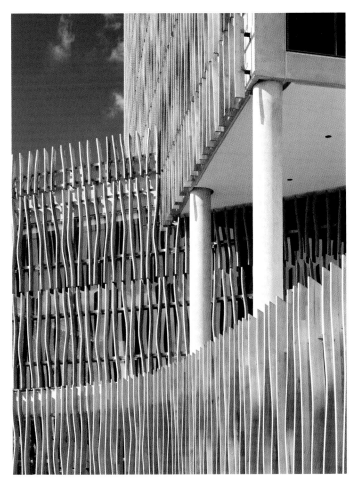

Aerial view of the Census Headquarters. The low buildings are pulled apart to allow natural light to permeate the interior.

Sections.
1 Remote delivery facility
2 Cafeteria
3 Office
4 Training center
5 Fitness center
6 Health unit
7 Library
8 Courtyard
9 Center spine
10 Parking

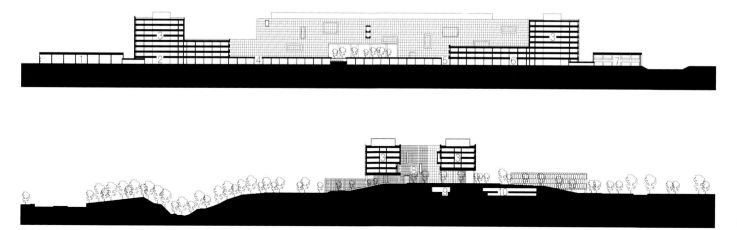

View of the courtyard between the bar buildings.

View of the courtyard from the east.

View of the auditorium from the north. Various volumes project from the west facade.

The main visitor lobby.

View of a community area. These two-story facilities support collaboration and communication with meeting areas, pantries, and stairs. Bright colors set these spaces off from the rest of the interior landscape.

View of an open-plan office with brise-soleil.

Plan, typical floor.

Plan, ground floor.
 1 Remote delivery facility
 2 Cafeteria
 3 Conference center
 4 Training center
 5 Auditorium
 6 Credit union
 7 Lobby
 8 Fitness center
 9 Healthcare
10 Café
11 Library
12 Street

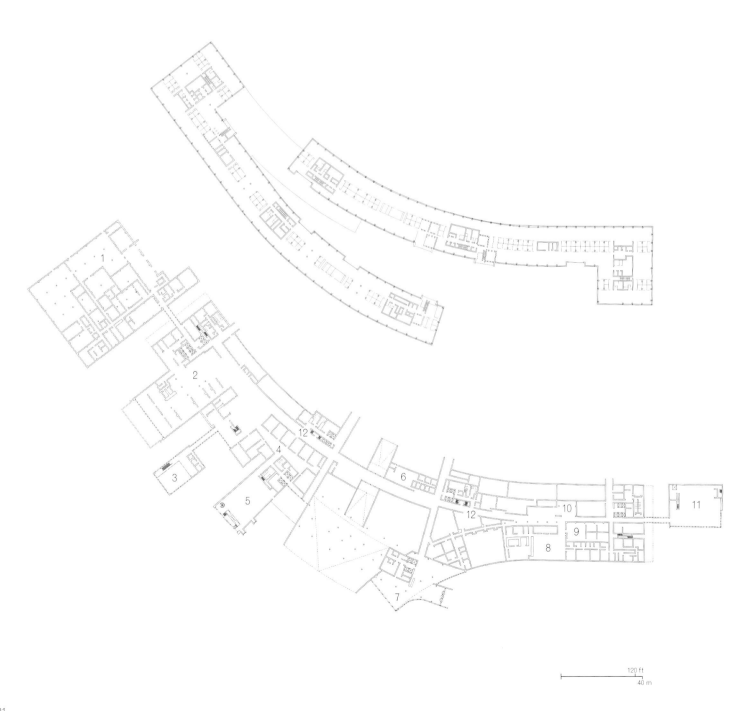

View of the internal street from the cafeteria. This public passageway, which links the amenities on the ground floor with the parking garage, ties together the headquarters complex.

View along the internal street. A digitally patterned artifical stone wall provides visual texture, breaking up the long corridor and reflecting natural light from above.

Views of the conference center. The center extends from the west side of the building and has views of the adjacent wetland preserve.

The library.

The entrance to the auditorium, which is located on the ground floor just off the internal street.

Interior view of the auditorium.

Central Trust Bank: Bank Branch Prototype
Lee's Summit, Missouri, 2007

This bank branch is one in a series of prototypes designed by SOM for the Central Bank; the association between the two companies started in the 1960s. Three different kinds of branches—neighborhood, community, and regional—establish a consistent brand and physical identity for the bank in the Midwest.

The design for the neighborhood branch draws from the expansive feeling of the prairie so prevalent in this part of the United States. A glazed pavilion sits on a stone base; steel columns support a long planar roof that reiterates the linear horizon of the landscape. Inside, fully glazed public zones allow views and daylight, while glass walls with etched portions create privacy. Areas for private bank functions reside in a solid masonry bar. The prototype employs sustainable technologies to mitigate heat and light, with a perimeter sunshade around the entire building, high-performance glazing, and white roof.

Site plan. The traditional role of the bank has evolved as it has become a highly accessible feature on the suburban and rural streetscape.

1 Entry vestibule
2 Lobby seating
3 Open customer-service office area
4 Private office/conference room
5 Teller area
6 Drive-through banking/ATM lanes

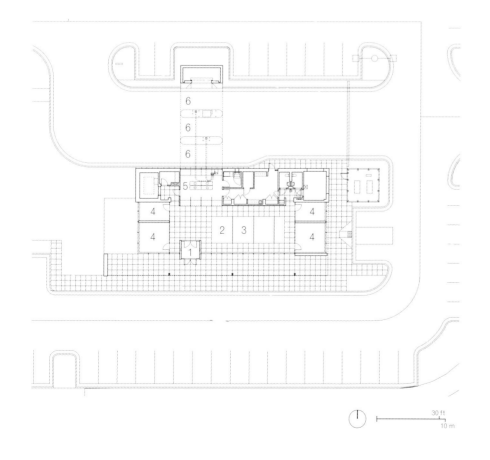

30 ft
10 m

View of the main entry. The project's strong horizontality refers to its Midwest location and emphasizes the relationship to the landscape. The deep south-facing overhang allows the interior spaces to have floor-to-ceiling glass.

Sections. The wood-paneled wall and masonry massing provide a backdrop for the glass-enclosed public areas and floating roof plane.

1 Entry vestibule
2 Main banking hall, offices beyond
3 Back of house and service area
4 Vehicle drive
5 Clerestory windows
6 Teller area
7 Cherry veneer panels
8 White brick masonry

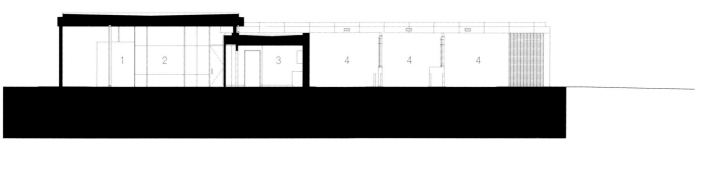

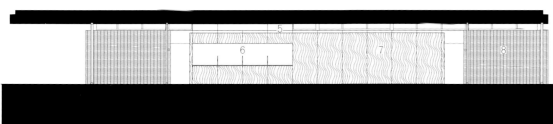

◁ View from the west. The cantilevered roof plane and extensive use of glazing create an open and inviting pavilion.

View of an executive office.

The main banking hall.

View of the private offices.

Beijing Finance Street
Beijing, China, 2007

This mixed-use development in the west side of the city forms a contemporary urban district and new financial center and includes an expansive park, much needed in this district of Beijing, which lacks open community space. SOM developed the master plan for the one-million-square-meter site with a series of buildings anchored by the fifteen-hectare park. The entire site is linked by a network of landscaped pathways, courtyards, and gardens as well as by an underground roadway that connects parking and services. In addition to planning, the firm also performed services for twenty-four buildings, the most prominent being the Ritz-Carlton hotel, the retail atrium, and the office tower complex.

Located at the southeastern edge of the development, the eighteen-story Ritz-Carlton faces the main avenue. The building's footprint and heavily glazed facade maximize panoramic views of the park and the Forbidden City. Glazed interior elements also forge a connection to the outdoors. Guests enter through a walled entry court, a private environment away from the street. Glass entries lead to the guest tower and ballroom, which are linked at the second floor by an enclosed transparent bridge. Other facilities include three restaurants, a 1,500-square-meter health club, and business center.

Adjacent to the hotel, the crescent-shaped retail atrium acts as an extension of the central park. Indoor and outdoor spaces offer entertainment, shopping, dining, and recreation. The main facade, which projects beyond the inclined glass roof, is divided into a series of modular compartments that display the shops, restaurants, and public spaces within, an effect intended to resemble a curio cabinet. Five terraced interior levels step down toward the ground, with view corridors to the park outside.

At the western edge of the site is the office tower complex, which is comprised of four buildings surrounding a glass-enclosed garden. Each building holds a corner: two twenty-four-story office towers, ovoid in plan, at the northeast and southwest; a four-story trading pavilion at the southeast; and a three-story conference center at the northwest. The towers, clad in glass and local stone, are oriented so that their short sides face east and west, minimizing their visual impact on the views from the park. The enclosed green space, known as the "all-seasons garden," draws on the concept of the Chinese courtyard. Its long-span roof is affixed to the superstructure of the towers.

Site plan.
1 Hotel
2 Retail atrium
3 Performing arts center
4 Ovoid tower
5 Trading pavilion
6 Conference center
7 Office tower
8 Central park
9 Finance Plaza
10 Low-rise residential
11 Fountain
12 Courtyard gardens

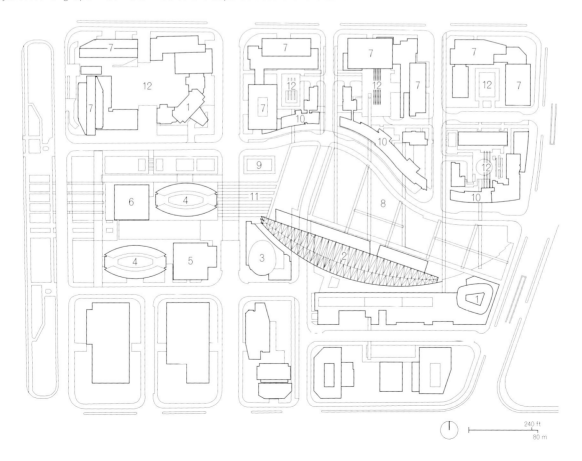

240 ft
80 m

Overall view of the district.

View of the fountain at Finance Plaza.

Section through retail atrium.
1 Terraced atrium levels
2 Retail
3 Service and parking
4 Parking
5 Health club

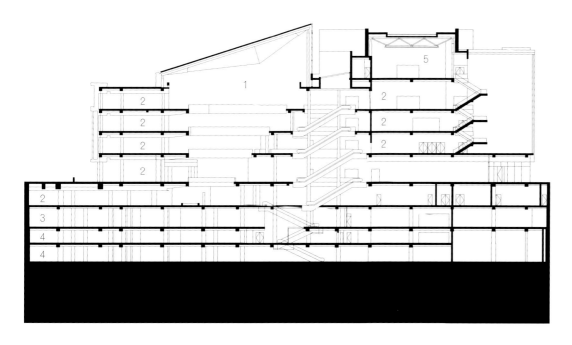

Plan, typical hotel tower level.
Plan, ground level.
1 Hotel
2 Hotel entry court
3 Health club
4 Retail atrium
5 Performing arts center
6 Performing arts lobby

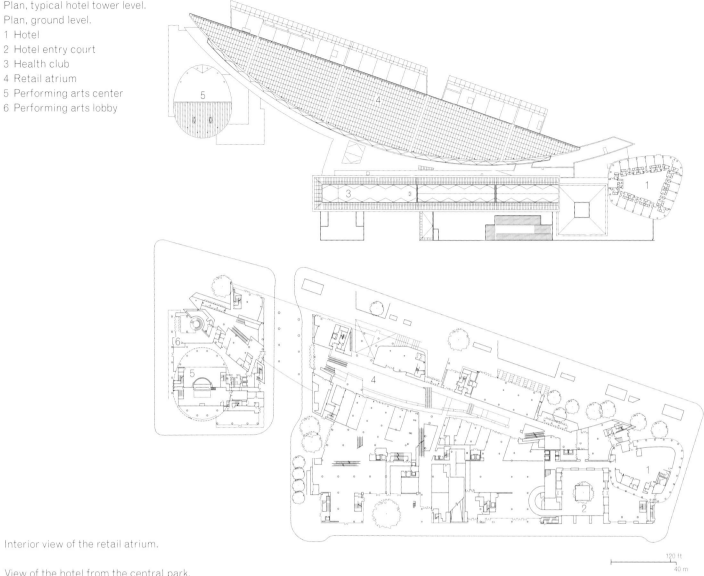

Interior view of the retail atrium.

View of the hotel from the central park.

120 ft
40 m

View of the ovoid office towers from the central park.

View of the stone screen at the base of one of the towers.

Section.
A South tower
B North tower
1 Trading floors
2 Executive club
3 Lobby
4 Restaurants
5 Café
6 All-seasons garden
7 Parking

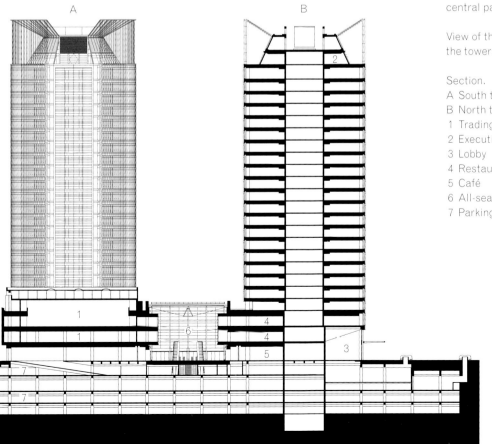

Plan, typical tower level.
Plan, ground level.
 1 North tower typical office level
 2 South tower typical office level
 3 North tower lobby
 4 South tower lobby
 5 Trading pavilion lobby
 6 Conference center lobby
 7 Banking hall
 8 Café
 9 Retail
10 All-seasons garden
11 Fountains

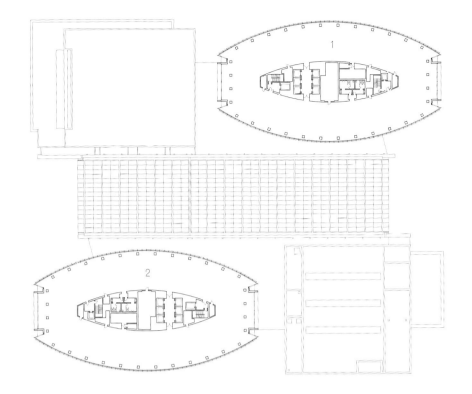

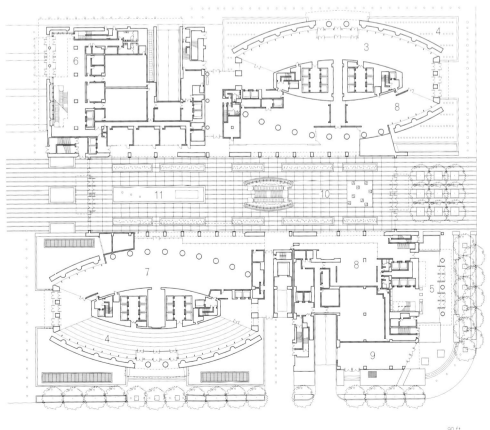

201 Bishopsgate and Broadgate Tower
London, United Kingdom, 2008

Built as part of London's Broadgate Development, which surrounds Liverpool Street Station, the project consists of two primary buildings, both located above active rail lines: 201 Bishopsgate, a low-rise horizontal structure of fifty-two thousand square meters, and Broadgate Tower, a thirty-five-story office building of fifty-five thousand square meters. A street-level wedge-shaped galleria runs between the two structures. Protected from the elements, this skylit public retail space serves as a pedestrian passageway between the Broadgate complex and Liverpool Street Station.

While the buildings and galleria read as a unified composition, each component maintains a separate identity. Broadgate Tower has a stepped profile formed by its vertical masonry cores and curtain wall with large-scale stainless-steel X-bracing. The first three floors house a triple-height entrance lobby; the levels above provide approximately four hundred thousand square feet of office space. The building has an A-frame structure that spans the underground rail tracks and helps form the retail galleria.

Two twelve-story bar buildings, also clad in stainless steel and fritted glass, comprise 201 Bishopsgate. The straight bar is angled in response to Broadgate Tower, forming one side of the galleria, and the other bar follows the slight bend of Primrose Street. In the center is a thirteen-story glass-enclosed atrium. The height and massing of 201 Bishopsgate respect the historic view corridor between King Henry's Mound and Saint Paul's Cathedral.

View of the south facade from Primrose Street. ▷ The A-frame struts, which straddle the railway below, create open space for the landscaped retail galleria between the two buildings.

Section.
 A Broadgate Tower
 B 201 Bishopsgate
 1 Underground railway tracks
 2 Skylight
 3 201 Bishopsgate atrium lobby
 4 Retail galleria
 5 A-frame strut
 6 Broadgate Tower atrium lobby
 7 Street-level retail
 8 Mechanical
 9 Typical office floor
10 Elevator lobby

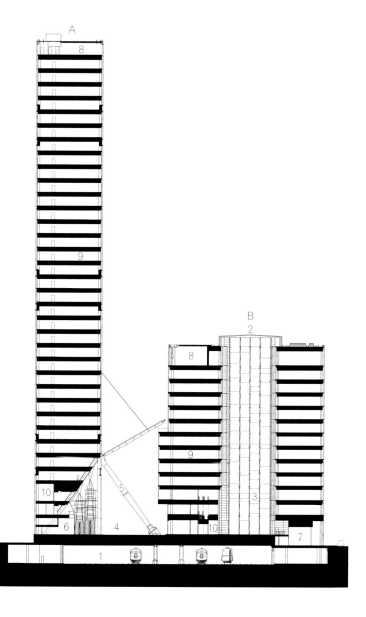

◁ View of Broadgate Tower from the north. The
X-bracing of the tower stands out against the
transparent and energy-efficient curtain wall
system.

Plan, typical floor.
Plan, site/ground level.
 A Broadgate Tower
 B 201 Bishopsgate
 1 Pedestrian plaza
 2 Retail galleria
 3 Street-level retail
 4 Main lobby
 5 Green wall and lawn
 6 North planter
 7 Worship Street bridge
 8 Norton Folgate
 9 Primrose Street
10 Boardwalk House
11 Exchange House

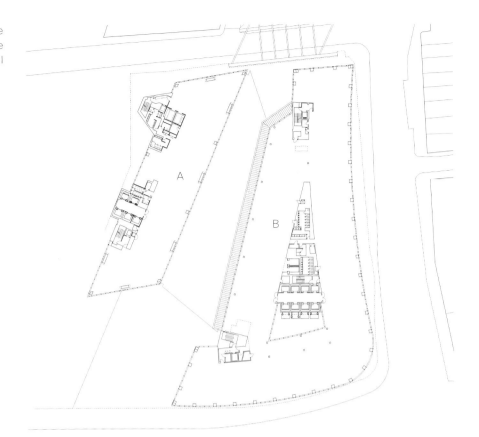

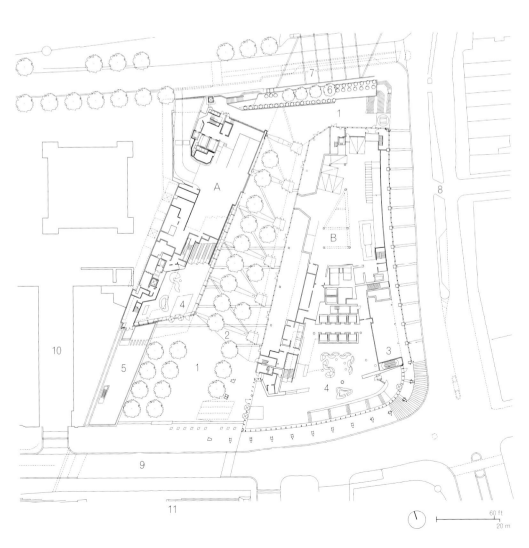

Memorial Sloan-Kettering: Mortimer B. Zuckerman Research Center
New York, New York, 2008

Located on a dense site on Manhattan's Upper East Side, the Mortimer B. Zuckerman Research Center resolves Memorial Sloan-Kettering's persistent shortage of research space while responding to the long-term planning study of the campus developed by SOM. One side of the building incorporates a rectory for an adjacent Catholic church, and the other cantilevers over an existing laboratory building. This structure will be demolished once the main building is completed; in its place will be inserted a conference center and other support functions.

Because it is vertical rather than horizontal, the 692,000-square-foot research facility is a new model for an urban research building. The two main programs, laboratories and office, support, and interaction spaces, provide the organizational strategy for the building, dividing it into two distinct volumes. Between these components is circulation, which also affords some visual communication between floors. The spatial organization is expressed on the exterior by a full-height terra-cotta dividing wall. The modular design maximizes flexibility for future research.

The visually distinct building components present four very different faces to the surrounding neighborhood. The laboratory volume has a skin of transparent, translucent, and opaque scrims of glass etched with graduated densities of ceramic frit. Variations in the pattern and density of the layered frit glass modulate the amount of daylight within as well as the amount of light radiating from the building at night. The office volume is wrapped in clear glass, providing expansive views and a strong connection to the campus and the city beyond. Integrated exterior sun-control devices protect the building interior from glare and direct solar heat gain.

View from the south. ▷

Plan, ground floor.
1 Lobby
2 Auditorium
3 Conference room
4 Staff support area
5 Rectory
6 Loading/storage
7 Existing church

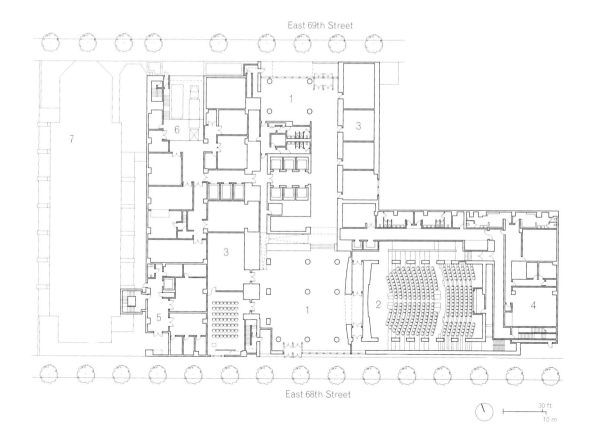

View from the northeast.

Section.
1 Lobby, service, conference center
2 Rectory, imaging, glasswash, mechanical
3 Wet/dry laboratory and support
4 Core support
5 Mechanical
6 Wet laboratory and support
7 Offices
8 Vivarium

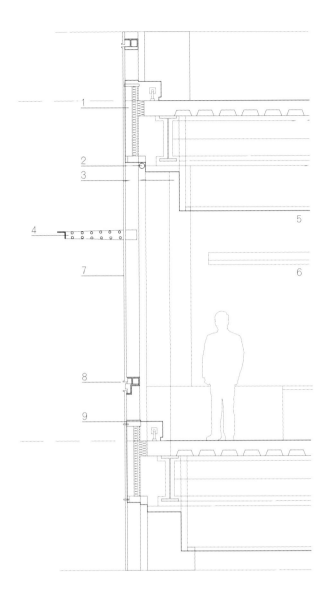

Section, typical office floor.
  1 Painted aluminum shadowbox
  2 Roll-down shade
  3 Painted drywall soffit and fascia
  4 Painted aluminum sunscreen
  5 Acoustical tile ceiling
  6 Pendant uplight fixture
  7 Insulated, low-E glass unit
  8 Painted aluminum mullion
  9 Painted aluminum convector cover

Exterior detail. The terra-cotta wall slips past
the transparent office volume.

View of integrated sun-shading devices on the
office volume.

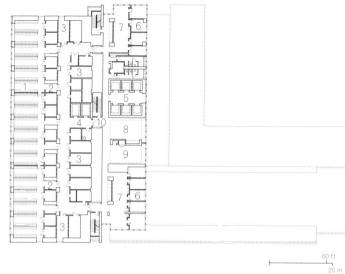

Plan, typical mid-rise floor.
Plan, typical tower floor.
 1 Laboratory wetbench
 2 Equipment alcove
 3 Procedure room
 4 Service elevator lobby
 5 Passenger elevator lobby
 6 Office
 7 Open office
 8 Lounge/interaction space
 9 Conference room
10 Interconnecting stair
11 Dry labs

Laboratory.

An interaction space in the office volume.

View from the west. ▷

U.S. Embassy
Beijing, China, 2008

The United States Embassy in Beijing occupies a ten-acre site in the city's Third Diplomatic Enclave. At five-hundred-thousand square feet, the project is one of the largest ever undertaken by the U.S. government. To serve the various users—State Department employees, diplomats, and the public——the site was divided into three areas, or neighborhoods. Each of these neighborhoods responds to the embassy's specific planning and security needs. The consular neighborhood, to the east, acts as the embassy's public face; it includes the consular pavilion and gardens. In the central zone is the professional neighborhood, the administrative and diplomatic core of the embassy. To the west is the community neighborhood, or social center, with a cafeteria and store for employees.

Within the three areas, eight low- and mid-rise buildings are united by a network of gardens. These structures are linked by courtyards and a central bamboo-lined walkway inspired by the traditional *hutongs*, or alleyways, of Beijing. The focal point is the eight-story office building, which has a skin of transparent, translucent, and opaque glass. The appearance of the glass changes with the sun over the course of a day; at night, it has a lantern-like glow. The two-story consular pavilion stands in a lotus water garden and has an expansive portico. The landscape elements of the embassy include gardens, courtyards, and wooden bridges, as well as a series of lotus ponds that purify storm water. The complex has an extensive public art program, with works by American and Chinese artists.

Using local, skilled labor allowed the use of finely detailed exterior concrete, providing human scale and rich texture. Almost all the materials were locally obtained and, where possible, recycled. Landscape, light, material, and craft support an overarching ethos of sustainability.

Site plan.
1 Office building
2 Consular pavilion
3 Marine quarters
4 Parking garage
5 Reception
6 Access control
7 Community room

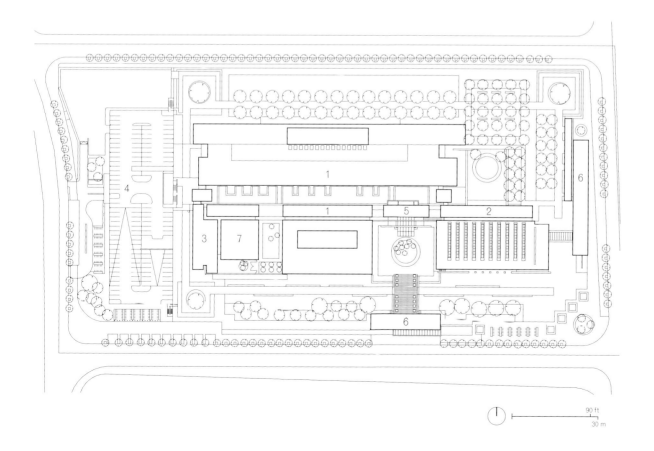

90 ft
30 m

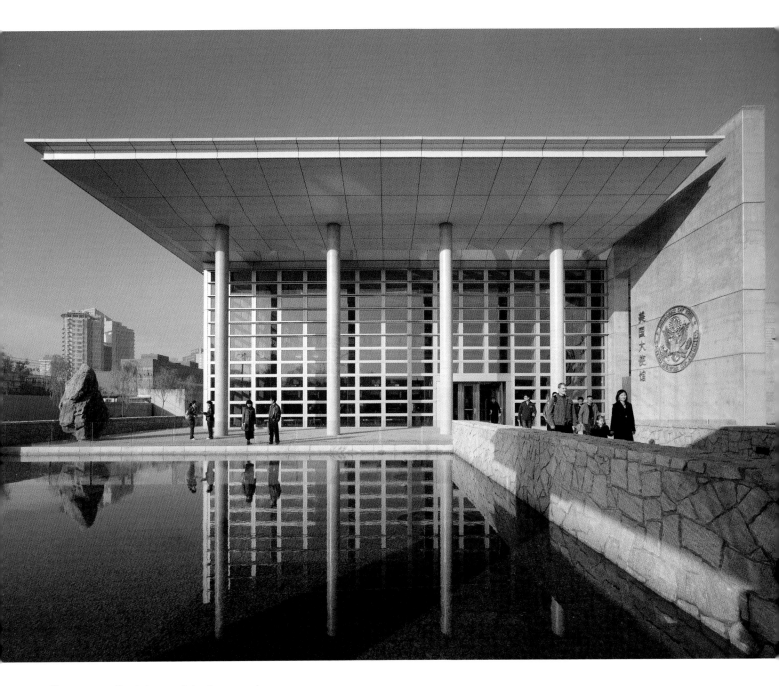

View across the lotus pool to the consular
pavilion entry.

◁ The atrium in the low-rise office building.

Facade of the mid-rise office building. The patterned, ceramic-frit-coated glass creates a sense of lightness and delicacy.

View to the east, with office buildings flanking the linear bamboo garden.

The visa hall in the consular pavilion.

View past the consular pavilion to the mid-rise office building. Jeff Koons's *Tulips* is set in the lotus pool.

Smithsonian National Museum of American History
Washington, D.C., 2008

Sited prominently on the National Mall in Washington, D.C., the Smithsonian's National Museum of American History is housed in a 1964 McKim, Mead & White building, the last project by this firm. Since the 350,000-square-foot building first opened as the Museum for History and Technology, it has been the foremost resource for visitors interested in exploring America's national identity through culture, history, and technology.

After more than forty years of operation, the flow of exhibits had become disorganized, public spaces had lost clarity, and the infrastructure and systems had deteriorated. In particular, the Star-Spangled Banner, the museum's most treasured artifact, was in dire need of conservation and a new exhibit space that would help preserve it.

SOM developed a plan that modernized the building's support systems, reorganized interior circulation, devised a central atrium with a new skylight and a grand staircase to connect the museum's first and second floors, and created a dramatic new gallery for the Star-Spangled Banner. The design brings the urban context into the building with a glazed perimeter of circulation galleries that provide views of the capital. The city's monuments become visual markers and a means of orientation for the visitors within.

The centerpiece of the newly open central core is the soaring Abstract Flag, a design based on the concept and physics of a waving flag. This forty-foot-long mirror polycarbonate sculpture is installed above the entrance to the gallery that features the newly preserved Star-Spangled Banner. Inside this gallery is an enormous hermetically sealed display case that protects the flag while providing maximum visibility for visitors. Lit by high-tech projectors in an otherwise black space, the fragile wool-and-cotton banner sits on an inclined aluminum table that allows museum curators and conservators to check the flag regularly. The ten-degree angle of elevation and low light levels protect the flag, yet the display is dramatic enough to evoke an atmosphere of "dawn's early light." The gallery has separate environmental systems that maintain a constant temperature of 68 to 72 degrees and relative humidity of 50 percent.

Plan, National Mall level.
1 Welcome center
2 Star-Spangled Banner chamber
3 Flag hall
4 Grand stair
5 Store

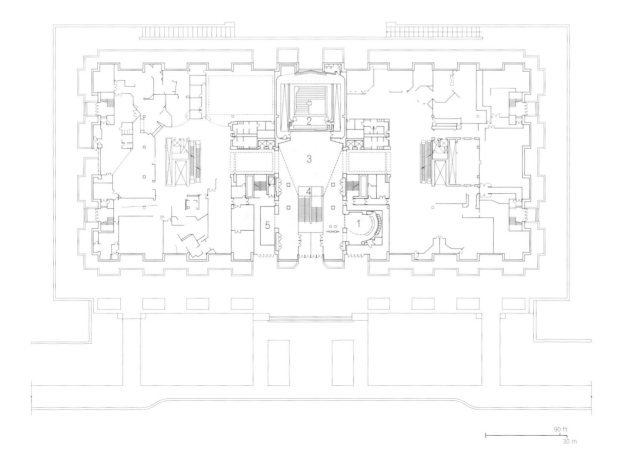

The glass grand stair that links the Constitution
Avenue level to the flag hall on the National
Mall level.

View of the flag hall with skylight, open balcony, and Mall entrance.

Section.
1 Star-Spangled Banner chamber
2 Abstract Flag
3 Flag hall
4 Grand stair
5 Skylight
6 National Mall entrance
7 Constitution Avenue entrance

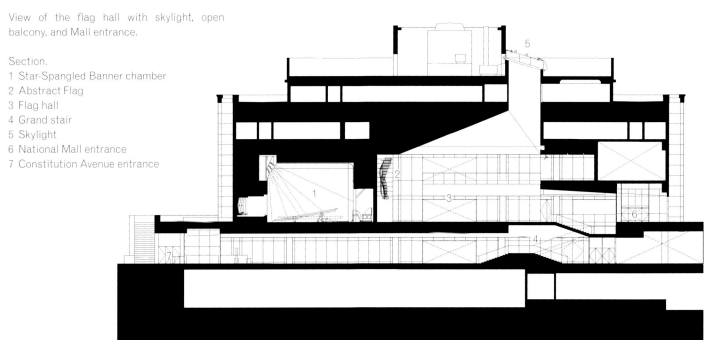

The Abstract Flag, a sculpture based on the mechanical form of a waving flag. The sculpture consists of 960 polycarbonate pixels in 15 rows.

Detail view of the Abstract Flag. The mirrored and translucent "pixels" of the sculpture form an ever-changing show of reflections and light.

View of the Star-Spangled Banner from the wood-decked viewing gallery.

Cathedral of Christ the Light
Oakland, California, 2008

The Cathedral of Christ the Light provides a sanctuary in the broadest sense of the word. Located in downtown Oakland, this house of worship offers solace, spiritual renewal, and respite from the secular world. The cathedral employs a nonlinear approach to honor the church's two-thousand-year history without espousing a specific point of view. By stripping away traditional iconography, the design positions symbolic meaning within contemporary culture.

As its name suggests, the cathedral draws on the idea of light as a sacred phenomenon. Introduced in a poetic manner, indirect daylight ennobles modest materials—primarily wood, glass, and concrete. With the exception of evening activities, the 224,000-square-foot cathedral is lit entirely by daylight to create an extraordinary level of luminosity.

SOM employed renewable materials in an innovative way, minimizing the use of energy and natural resources and achieving the lightest ecological footprint possible. An advanced version of an ancient Roman technique, thermal inertia, maintains the interior climate with mass and radiant heat. Douglas fir, obtained through sustainable harvesting processes, is used for the interior; aesthetically pleasing, economically sound, and structurally forgiving, the wood adds warmth, while its elasticity allows for the bending and returning of shape during seismic activity. Through the use of advanced seismic techniques, including base isolation, the structure is able to withstand a thousand-year earthquake.

View of the cathedral from Lake Merritt. The ▷ building sits on a poured-in-place concrete podium.

Site plan.
 1 Ramp
 2 Entrance
 3 Sanctuary
 4 Courtyard
 5 Shop
 6 Café
 7 Lake Merritt

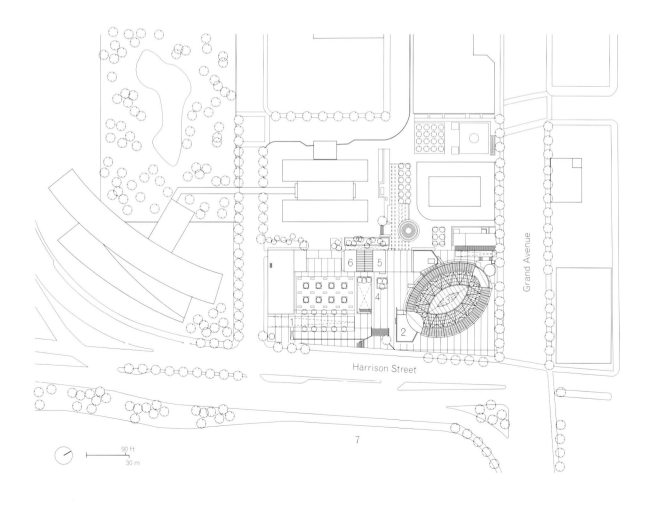

Grand Avenue

Harrison Street

7

90 ft
30 m

◁ View from the altar toward the Alpha Window.
The sanctuary is 106 feet high.

View along the concrete reliquary wall. The
apertures in the wall lead to different chapels.
The louvers above are Douglas fir, and the
curved pews are made of red oak.

Plan, sanctuary.
1 Entry
2 Baptismal font
3 Sanctuary
4 Altar
5 Bishop's chair
6 Reredos
7 Side chapel
8 Reconciliation chapel
9 Sacristy

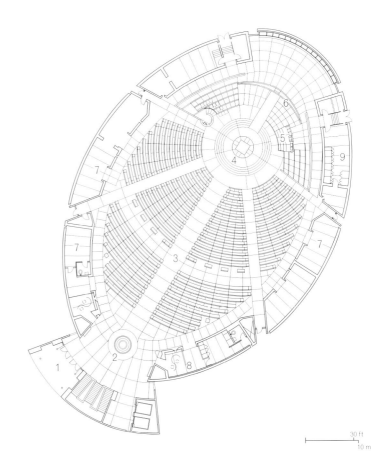

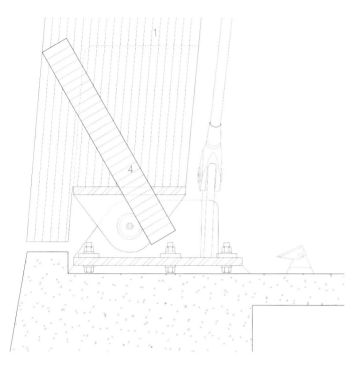

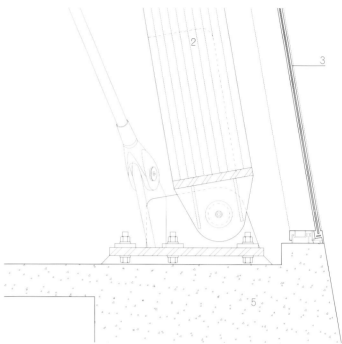

Detail of wood structure and curtain wall at top of reliquary wall.
1 Curved glue-laminated timber
2 Glue-laminated timber
3 Laminated glass enclosure
4 Glue-laminated louver
5 Concrete reliquary wall

◁ View of the baptismal font and entry at the Alpha Wall. The aluminum-paneled Alpha Window is above.

◁ The mausoleum entrance.

View of a side chapel within the reliquary wall.

The mausoleum. The catafalque corresponds in plan with the altar in the sanctuary above.

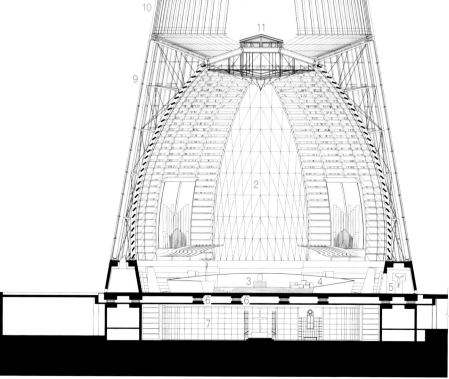

Sections through the sanctuary and mausoleum. The building sits on thirty-six friction pendulum base isolators located beneath the sanctuary floor slab. The friction pendulums allow the structure to move with seismic activity.

1 Sanctuary
2 Omega Window
3 Altar
4 Reredos
5 Side chapel
6 Friction pendulum base isolators
7 Mausoleum
8 Catafalque
9 Support ribs
10 Steel finials
11 Oculus ceiling

◁ View from the Eucharist Chapel of the reredos, which curves behind the altar.

The Omega Window.

Pages 262–263:
View from the courtyard.

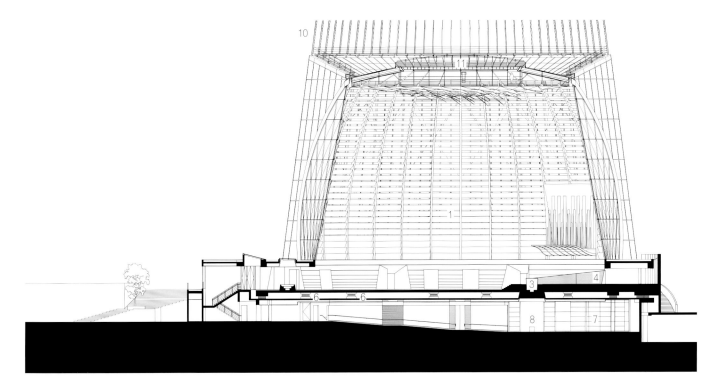